Are There Bun Shops in the Jungles of India?

AND OTHER SECRET STORIES FROM HISTORY

Nandini Nayar is the author of over 60 books for children of all ages. Although her postal code says she lives in Hyderabad, in actual fact Nandini inhabits several worlds. Every morning, she sets out on voyages of discoveries, and returns with stories about animals and children, trees and seas. It was on one of these journeys that Nandini stumbled across tales about the people and animals in this book. For more information, please visit www.nandininayar.in

Are There Bun Shops in the Jungles of India?

AND OTHER SECRET STORIES FROM HISTORY

NANDINI NAYAR

Illustrations by Damini Gupta

hachette INDIA

First published in 2023 by Hachette India
(Registered name: Hachette Book Publishing India Pvt. Ltd)
An Hachette UK company
www.hachetteindia.com

1

ISBN 978-93-5731-248-6

Hachette Book Publishing India Pvt. Ltd
4th & 5th Floors, Corporate Centre
Plot No. 94, Sector 44, Gurugram – 122003, India

Typeset by Manmohan Kumar, Delhi

Printed and bound in India
by Manipal Technologies Limited

MIX
Paper from responsible sources
FSC™ C043100
www.fsc.org

For the animals of the world

CONTENTS

IF YOU'RE WONDERING WHAT THIS BOOK IS *ACTUALLY* ABOUT...

Imagine yourself back in the eighteenth century, floating high above the blue waters of the ocean that lay between India and England. There, far below, is a ship bound for England. Let's swoop down on it and see what it carries. Ooh, what's this? These are rolls of brightly coloured silk and the finest cotton fabric. The smell scenting the air comes from the sacks of spices. There are piles of green cardamom and spicy pepper. You are just about to open the next sack, when you hear a growl. You look up and see a tiger, its eyes glowing in the dark. You freeze, heart thumping loudly, and wonder if the tiger is going to spring on you. That's when you see the bars that hold it back and realize that the tiger is in a cage. You sigh in relief. The next minute you wonder – why is there a tiger on the ship?

The English came to India in the 1600s, in search of spices. The East India Company was set up so that English merchants could trade in India, and carry spices and other treasures back home. The company officials negotiated with the rulers of the time, seeking permission to trade. Soon, the company had spread its trading operations around the country. Winning the Battle of Plassey in 1757 changed the very nature of the East India Company's presence in India. The company now played a significant role in ruling different princely states around the country. They adopted a series of treaties to bring more such states under their control.

However, the people of India were unhappy with the interference of the British and this found expression in 1857 when the Indian sepoys employed by the British rose in protest. Although the protest began in Meerut, it rapidly spread to other cities. Variously called the Sepoy Mutiny and the First War of Independence, this uprising was only subdued in 1858. The East India Company was abolished and it was decided that India would henceforth be directly ruled by the British Crown.

India thus became a part of the British Empire and this resulted in many changes. Now, administrative officials were appointed by the British government and sent to India. These young men who travelled to India were selected on the basis of their performance in the Indian Civil Service exam. They were often posted to remote locations in the hinterland of India, with very little social life to keep them occupied. Many of them turned to hunting, travelling long distances in search of tigers and bears.

This new generation of Englishmen felt the same awe that the early travellers to India had felt, when they saw forests swarming with tigers, lions, elephants, and a host of other animals and brightly coloured birds. Why, India was home to the amazing rhinoceros, which had never been seen in England. The seventeenth century was the Age of Discovery in England, as people travelled around the world, visiting new places and learning about the people, their customs and their unique flora and fauna.

The establishment of the East India Company offered them easy and continuous access to the natural wealth of India. A letter was written to the directors of the company, asking if a collector of animals could be sent on one of their ships. The company was unwilling to take responsibility of the collector and said so. Instead, it suggested that the sailors on ships returning from India could bring back animals and birds.

This was how animals travelled from India to England. Animals were taken as companions for the sailors, as gifts for important people in England and also to be sold there for a tidy profit. Many animals died in the violent process of trapping. Several others died on the long journey. These were immediately put into spirits, so the naturalists waiting eagerly in England could dissect them and learn about them. The animals that survived the journey were sold to menageries and displayed to the eager public of England.

Some of these animals were exhibited in inns and at street corners to help the owners earn some money. George Wombwell, the owner of one of the most successful travelling menageries, was actually a cobbler. On a whim, he bought two boa constrictors from a sailor at the London docks and began to display them. This earned him so much money that Wombwell bought more animals and set up his own travelling menagerie.

How did the elephant, used to living with its clan, react to the lonely life in the cage of a menagerie? What about the tiger, denied the instinctive hunting of its food in the jungles and restricted by the bars of its cage? Monkeys and parrots, used to the hot climate of India, perished in large numbers on the journey to England. There were stories of small animals and birds that curled up in the corners of their cages, distressed by the sudden change in their circumstances.

This collection of stories emerged from vast archives about the animals that were transported out from India, and questions about their adjustment to a life in cages and the utterly callous practices in menageries.

Each of these stories is based on a real animal that was snatched away from its life in the jungles of

India, and thrust into a completely new and merciless environment. The people who write the letters, however, are purely imaginary. Reading about these animals made me think about things fair and unfair, and to dream of a future where we would treat every living creature with kindness.

I hope you will feel the same way too.

NOTE: Animals have been referred to as he or she, wherever the author has been able to ascertain this from the records.

CAN WILD ANIMALS CLIMB STAIRS?

When someone says 'zoo', you probably think of wide-open spaces, a large number of trees, perhaps a picnic somewhere. And of course, a lot of walking around to look at the animals. But this was not always the case, particularly in England.

The earliest collection of animals in England was located in the Tower of London. The other well-known collection was displayed on the upper floor of a building called the Exeter Exchange. A businessman named Thomas Clark sold cutlery and other home items here. But sometime in the 1770s, he used the upper floor to display animals, usually from India and Africa. This was the beginning of the Exeter Exchange menagerie, which attracted many visitors eager to see the strange animals.

Did anyone ever wonder about how the animals climbed the stairs to the first floor? There are no records of any curiosity about this. But if someone had asked this question, it would have been a child! And this is what that smart child would probably have done – written a letter to Mr Thomas Clark, the owner of the menagerie and the only person who could answer his questions about animals and stairs.

10 September 1787

Dear Mr Clark,

My name is George Thomas Landmann. Last week, my father took me to see the wild animals at the Exeter Change menagerie. I know that the Exeter Change menagerie is famous. It is listed in a book about the places to see in London, and my aunt, who lives in the countryside, has the book. She brought it with her when she came to visit us last month and looked at it every time she wanted to decide where she wanted to go. She said the place was called Exeter *Exchange* menagerie and Papa said it was not. That it was Exeter *Change* menagerie.

She took my cousins to see the animals there and came back with such stories! They said the lions had roared at them, the snake had stared at them and the llama had spat at them. They even showed me how the animals roared and growled and paced around. My aunt said again and again that they had enjoyed the visit to the Exeter Exchange very much indeed.

As soon as they left, Papa said that he was taking me to see the animals. I had heard so much about the animals

Aunty was right, after all! The building in the heart of London was called the Exeter Exchange. The three-storey structure was built around 1670 as a place of trade. It had a bazaar with many stalls on the ground floor. The menagerie occupied only the upper two floors, but soon, the building was known for the collection of animals displayed there. The name was shortened to Exeter 'Change by the locals.

and the 'Change, but no one had said *where* the 'Change was. Or where the animals lived. All the animals I had seen lived on farms. There were a few farms beyond our house, and I often saw large herds of their cows go plodding past. So, I was very surprised when Papa led me down the Strand. I could see signposts announcing that Charing Cross lay just ahead. Where exactly was this menagerie?

Then we stopped on the street, and I looked up to see a three-storey building. There were people walking past, and carts and carriages rumbled behind us. But I heard nothing because I was filled with astonishment. There, on the building, were large pictures of animals.

There was a big sign too, announcing that this was the Exeter Exchange menagerie. I was too surprised to say anything, but I heard Papa mutter that it was always the

These big images of animals were called 'daubs' and were large, coloured pictures meant to attract passers-by.

'Change and only people who didn't live in London called it the Exchange. I knew he was annoyed that my aunt had been right, and he had been wrong. It doesn't feel good to be wrong and I wanted to say something to my father. At that moment, a man dressed in a red uniform, with gold bits flashing in the sun, began to call out loudly.

'Walk *up*! Walk *up*! And see the CURIOSITIES and CREATURES – all alive! Alive O! Walk *up*! Now's your time. Only a shilling. Ladies and gentlemen, these animals have been exhibited at Court, before the KING and all the royal family! Walk *up*! Walk *up*!'

Imagine hearing a man in a gorgeous crimson-and-gold uniform say these words! Wouldn't you be tempted to rush up the stairs to see these animals? These men were appointed by the menagerie to grab the attention of people walking by.

There was a pole near him, with a brightly coloured bird swinging on it, and now the bird added its loud cries to the man's voice. I was filled with a burning curiosity to see these creatures the man was talking about. And when Papa pulled me along, I went willingly. We walked through a covered passage, with stalls on both sides of it. I looked at the glass cases in these stalls eagerly. Surely, the lions and tigers were not stuffed in there?

They were not. Instead, I saw bottles of perfume, cutlery, even toys displayed there. Had Papa played a trick on me and brought me here to shop? Then Papa led me up some stairs and I was glad to get away from that gloomy, dirty place, with people crowding around to buy the dullest things. As we went up the stairs, I heard a loud squawking, and leaving Papa behind, I hurried on. And there was the entrance to the menagerie! Just inside the doors were brightly coloured birds, squawking and calling to each other. I was happy to stand looking at them while Papa went away to pay the admission.

'Walk up! Walk up!' I heard someone shout. 'Come and see the lion roar!' The lion had a magnificent roar, loud and deep. It made a few people gasp in fear and I saw some little boys hide behind their mothers. The lion's roar set the tiger off. Soon it was snarling and walking with tight, angry steps round its cage. Its tail lashed the bars of the

The animals needed someone to feed them, clean out their cages and keep an eye on them. This was the keeper. The keepers soon learnt how to deal with the animals in their care, and what they liked and disliked. It was they who knew when the animal was ill or angry.

cage and I saw someone put out a hand to touch it. Just in time the keeper shouted a warning, and the hand was snatched back. There was a leopard too, hissing angrily, and across the room a cageful of monkeys chattered in excitement. People gasped and muttered, looking around the room at the restless flutter and scamper of animals. But I was puzzling over a question that had come to me as we had stood outside the building.

As soon as I had Papa's attention, I asked him how the lions, the tigers and the llamas had all walked up the stairs into the Exeter Exchange menagerie. Several people laughed at my question. But the keeper who heard it, didn't. Instead, he explained that the animals had been carried up the stairs in boxes or cages. And for the elephant, he said, a wooden board had been laid over the stairs. The elephant had walked up this board and into its cage.

I saw then that I had not asked the right question. *How* the animals came to the upper floor of the Exeter Exchange

Menagerie did not matter. *Why* had they been brought to the top floors of a building? *Why* had they been put in a crowded room, between walls, with a wooden floor under their feet and a sky of brown beams to look up at? True, there were some splashes of green where the walls had been painted with pictures of trees and bushes. But these were not real trees that the monkeys could climb or the birds could nest in. These were not leaves that could be plucked by the elephant, or turn black in winter and flutter to the ground.

The pictures painted on the walls were never meant to make the *animals* happy! They had been painted so that the people who came to see the animals could be fooled into thinking that they were in the middle of a forest. The animals, as you can see, mattered very little.

I knew that this question had never occurred to the keeper. And I knew that my father could not answer it. That is why I am writing to you, Mr Clark. You own the Exeter Exchange menagerie and all the animals in it. Why don't you let them live on a farm? They can feel the grass and enjoy the fresh breeze. The people who go to see them can also enjoy the experience.

This young visitor to the menagerie was way ahead of his time! But it was only when several others, who all believed that animals deserved better living conditions, came together, that the idea of a zoological garden was born. In 1828, Regent's Park Zoo was opened in London. In 1907, a German trader of wild animals, Carl Hagenback, introduced the world to a completely different way of viewing animals in captivity. The animals in his collection were not exhibited as prisoners but as 'free' creatures, separated from the humans by a deep moat. The current way of displaying animals is inspired by the Hagenback method.

I understand you have many things to attend to. Perhaps you have not had the time to think of what the animals in the menagerie need. Mr Clark, I have done your work for you. I thought about all the animals I had seen in your menagerie. I also thought about what they need, what they like and enjoy. I used these to plan a different kind of menagerie. I am happy to share my plan and explain it to you. I hope this finds favour with you and you move the animals to a place where they don't have to climb stairs.

I remain,

Your most obedient,

George Thomas Landmann

Qs and As

Didn't the people of England think it strange to have animals housed inside buildings?

No, they didn't. Do you know why? This was because the very first menagerie in England was housed in, not a field, not a park but in...the Tower of London! A menagerie meant a collection of wild animals. In the thirteenth century, people gifted the king of England wild animals from different countries. The king soon had lions, bears and even elephants. He sent these to the Tower of London, and that's where they stayed. By the eighteenth century, people were used to the idea of wild animals being kept inside buildings. So, when Thomas Clark decided to exhibit his collection in the Exeter Exchange, no one was surprised.

If you lived in eighteenth-century England, where would you have gone to see wild animals?

The rich people of England often had collections of exotic animals. We already know that the king of England was gifted animals. However, these collections were not open to the public; they could only be seen by members of the family and their friends. So, for people eager to see animals from the distant shores of Africa or India, the Exeter Exchange menagerie was the place to visit. The people of London and visitors to the city made it a point to visit the menagerie at the Exeter Exchange.

So what about the people who didn't live in London? For these people, there were menageries that travelled around the country. They gave them an opportunity to see animals from distant countries whose names they had only heard of. The animals travelled to remote villages and bustling market towns in caravans pulled by horses. These menageries were well advertised and attracted huge crowds of people eager to see these animals.

Sadly, though, very little thought was given to the animals that were the heroes of the menageries. They spent years in tiny cages with barely enough room to move. With no opportunity to get regular exercise, animals often became bad-tempered and developed health problems.

Wait, so does that mean that animals are still displayed inside buildings in England?

Oh, no! In 1826, a group of people set up the Zoological Society of London. In 1828, the Regent's Park Zoo (also called London Zoo) opened its doors to the public. Here, people could enjoy a walk through the garden while they looked at the animals. The animals were still in cages that were sometimes too small for them, but slowly things improved.

How wonderful! So, the Exeter Exchange menagerie moved to a garden?

The menagerie at Exeter Exchange continued in the city till 1830. That was when Edward Cross, the owner at the time, moved it to the Surrey Zoological Gardens.

What finally got the animals out of those dreadfully cramped rooms?

In 1816, a fire broke out in the building behind the Exeter Exchange menagerie. The fear was, what if it spread to the menagerie? The wild animals would then be on the loose in the city of London. It was a frightening thought. A few years later, the Exeter Exchange building was going to be demolished and so the animals were moved to the Surrey Zoological Gardens in 1831.

Strange but True

Kings and princes enjoyed watching wild animals fight. There are stories of lions and tigers being pitted against dogs or other animals. A duke who ordered a fight between a tiger and a stag was surprised when the stag defeated the tiger. The duke had a silver collar made for the stag and even granted it freedom, in appreciation of its courage.

SECRET POST

EDWARD CROSS: MENAGERIE OWNER

The menagerie of Edward Cross was visited by several 'celebrities' of the time, including the poets William Wordsworth and Lord Byron. Scientists also came to the menagerie to study the animals. One of them was the acclaimed zoologist J.E. Grey who named the *Rhinoceros 'crossii'* (or the Sumatran rhinoceros) in Edward Cross's honour. Among the other famous visitors was the painter Jacques-Laurent Agasse, who painted Cross (in top hat, see left) with a giraffe.

A JOURNEY OF SORROWS

There were several things to worry the owner of a menagerie in eighteenth-century England. Many of the animals for their collections came from the forests of India. They were captured in the jungles of India and transported to the nearest port in the country. Then they began the long sea voyage to England, which could take up to six months! Many of these animals died of ill-health or stress on the ship itself. Birds, sometimes, died of sorrow, refusing to eat and wasting away. Carnivores needed large amounts of fresh meat.

A tiger donated by the Governor of Bombay to the Liverpool Zoological Park and Gardens ate 16 sheep on the journey. Sometimes, the fresh meat for the animals ran out and, with nothing to feed the animals, the only option was to kill them.

SHELLFISH WOODS

Exeter Exchange in 1826, with the menagerie in its upper floor

2

WHY WAS THE RHINOCEROS DUG UP?

Menagerie owners were always looking for new animals to display. And Gilbert Pidcock, who worked with Thomas Clark and later took over the Exeter Exchange menagerie, was no different. So, he was thrilled when he got a rhinoceros from India in 1790.

Most people in the country had never seen a rhinoceros before and huge crowds flocked to the menagerie. Sadly, the rhinoceros died in just three years. But that was not the end of this unusual animal for the menagerie owner. Gilbert Pidcock, it was reported, dug up the body of the dead rhinoceros!

Why would he do that? Of what use was a dead rhinoceros? These were the questions that occurred to young Susan Oldsmith and that she demanded answers to!

17 September 1793
Dear Mr Pidcock,
I beg your pardon for writing to you. I never would have dared to do it if it were not for my friend Betty. Oh, and Billy too, who is the boy who delivers meat and is also our friend.

I am Susie, the youngest kitchen maid in a grand house that is in the heart of London. All day long, I hurry hot dishes of food from the kitchen to the dining table, and carry dirty plates away from the table. Cook and Butler and James the footman always warn me to be careful and frown horribly if I stumble or the plates jiggle the tiniest bit in my hands. But I pay them no heed because my heart is full of joy. And it is all because of you, my dear Mr Pidcock. And of course, the real unicorn. My wonderful, magical unicorn.

My gran, she told me stories about the unicorn. It was enchanted, she said, and it changed every life it touched. Two years ago, I was thinking of my gran. I was missing her and my mother and all my little brothers and sisters. I had missed them from the moment I had reached London. But that day was 5 June 1790, and it was my birthday. And that somehow made the pain sharper. You see, there was no one to remember that it was my birthday, or to give me a smile and a hug. I had only been in London a few days and knew no one. Oh,

Susie's magical unicorn was actually a rhinoceros!

England's first rhinoceros arrived in August 1684. This was a female rhinoceros who came from Machilipatnam in India. However, there are no details recorded about who captured it and how. The owners, who had hoped to sell it, were disappointed when this didn't happen. With a view to earning their money back, they then displayed the rhinoceros. For an additional fee, people were even allowed to ride the animal. The rhinoceros, though, didn't live very long and died in September 1686.

there were plenty of people in the house. But I was too shy to talk to them.

Two days later, I was thinking of Gran's unicorn and wishing it would fly into my little room at the top of the house. I imagined touching the horn and making a wish. The horn, Gran had told me, was where all the magic of the unicorn was stored. What would I wish for?

I was trying to decide when Cook sent me out to throw some garbage. I opened the kitchen door and stepped into the narrow alley. And there, stuck on the wall, was the picture of a unicorn. I stared at it, my heart thumping in excitement and hope. This was *my* unicorn,

The last rhinoceros to be seen by the people of England was Clara, in 1756. Clara was born in Assam in India and orphaned at an early age. She arrived in Rotterdam, Holland, when she was three years old and spent the next 17 years of her life touring Europe. And now, over 30 years later, the people of England had an opportunity to see a rhinoceros again. They flocked in large numbers to see it, to marvel at its thick skin divided into sections. But it was its single horn that made them refer to the animal as a unicorn.

the one Gran had told me about. There, at the end of its nose, was a horn. It was small, that horn, more like a stub. But that didn't matter. Because I knew it was a horn. And that it had magic in it. Below the picture were the words, 'The Real Unicorn or the Rhinoceros'.

It had reached London on 5 June. That was my birthday, the day I turned ten.

I had to go into the house because I could hear Cook shouting for me. But I could not stop thinking of the unicorn and feeling delighted bursts of hope at all the magic it was going to bring into my life. And do you know, Mr Pidcock, that unicorn got to work at once! The first magical thing that happened was finding a friend in that cold, unfriendly house in London.

> The rhinoceros came from India and was bought by Thomas Clark, who ran the Exeter Exchange menagerie, for 700 pounds. The male rhinoceros was only two years old and therefore it had a short horn.

My first friend was Betty, the girl who had been the youngest kitchen maid before I came to the house in London. I had not said a word to her in all the days I had been there. But now, I was so eager to learn about the unicorn that I stopped being scared and asked the first person I saw. That was Betty, hurrying along the passage carrying a tray loaded with dishes. She didn't laugh at me when I asked her about the unicorn or tell me I was silly. Instead, she took me to meet Billy. She said he knew of everything that happened in London and was sure to know something about my unicorn.

She was right. Billy delivers meat to many houses in London. He keeps his eyes and ears open, and picks up the smallest crumbs of information. He told us many things about the unicorn. He said it had travelled all the way from India. Betty and I stared when he said that because we thought only soft muslin cloth came from India. Billy was very kind and didn't laugh at us. He said many animals lived in the jungles of India. My unicorn had lived there too, until it had been put on a ship and brought all the way to London. It was going to be displayed in the Exeter Exchange menagerie for people to look at. And if we wanted to see it, all we had to do was pay the admission fee and enter the menagerie! But, Mr Pidcock, neither Betty nor I had any money.

People who wished to see the rhinoceros had to pay the admission fee of one shilling. This was a large amount, particularly for two young maids. In later years, menageries had different rates of admission for the rich, for working-class people and a discounted rate for children.

Every penny we earned was sent home to help care for the younger children. We decided that the only thing to do was save whatever little we could and then to go and see the unicorn. The salary of the two youngest kitchen maids working in a grand house in London is very little, Mr Pidcock.

Two years passed, and we had still not managed to save money for our admission to the menagerie. In this time, Betty and I became close friends. She told me about her brothers and her baby sister. And I told her all the stories Gran had told me about the unicorn. Soon, everyone in the kitchen had heard these stories. The butler, Mr Thomas, who always looks so stern and serious, surprised me very much by asking me about the unicorn.

That was when Billy brought news that you had bought the unicorn, Mr Pidcock. And that it would now be taken around the country, and shown at every village and town on the way. People all over the country, Billy told me, were eager to see the rhinoceros. Why, the queen was too. Billy told us how the queen had asked for the unicorn to be taken to Windsor so that everyone in the palace could see it. I do wish, Mr Pidcock, that you had not done that.

The members of the royal family often went to look at unusual animals. Queen Victoria enjoyed lion-taming performances, even staying on to watch them being fed. The animals were kept hungry for 36 hours so she could enjoy the sight of them tearing ravenously into their food. Sometimes, menagerie owners were invited by members of the royal family to show a particular animal. On 3 June 1793, Pidcock took his rhinoceros to Windsor where King George, Queen Charlotte and their children enjoyed the experience of seeing the unusual animal.

If you hadn't taken the rhinoceros there, perhaps it would have been alive still. But you did, and two days later the unicorn was dead. And I had never even set eyes on it!

It was the darkest hour of my life. I wept at my hopelessness, I cried for all the dashed dreams. I think it was my eyes, red from weeping, that the Master noticed at dinner. Betty says the Master and Mistress don't look at us. But they certainly must have heard me sniffing, she says.

Anyway, the Master asked me what was wrong. I was just getting ready to say nothing was, when Betty burst into speech. She told him about the unicorn and how long I had dreamt of seeing it. The Master was astonished. The rhinoceros, he muttered to himself, remarkable, remarkable. I could see that Betty had been hoping for something more than that and was disappointed. But nothing mattered to me – not the Master's kindness nor the rough hug Cook gave me that night.

To our surprise, the Master did not forget what Betty had told him about the rhinoceros. He brought the newspaper to the table and read out any news about it. We knew that the rhinoceros had been buried. Now we learnt that it had been dug up. Why had this happened? Why could you, Mr Pidcock, not let the poor beast rest in peace?

We soon found out! And once again the information came from the Master's newspaper. The rhinoceros had

Menagerie owners used a variety of ways to attract the attention of the public to their animals. For example, the public was informed that the rhinoceros came from the 'empire of the GREAT Mogul' and had been presented to an English nobleman by 'an Eastern Rajah'. Other advertisements talked about the size of the animal and how much it had cost, or stressed the fact that this was an unusual beast.

been dug up, the Master told us, for its skin and bones. These would be used to stuff the animal. This stuffed rhinoceros, the newspaper announced, was on display at the Exeter Exchange menagerie.

Go and see your rhinoceros, the Master told Betty and me, pushing something into my hand. I opened my hand and there, in my palm, lay a shiny coin. There was enough there for three people to go to the menagerie.

So, Betty, Billy and I went one afternoon. Everyone in the kitchen gathered at the door to wave us off. Betty and Billy wandered around the menagerie, looking at the animals. They laughed at the monkeys and stared at the tigers pacing up and down and round and round in their cages. They came up to me again and again, trying to drag me to see the lions, the tigers and the colourful birds. But I was happy where I was, looking at the unicorn

The people of England had to wait till 1799 to see a live rhinoceros again. Sadly, the young Indian rhinoceros, healthy enough on the voyage from India, developed breathing difficulties in just a few months and died in early 1800.

Those who had missed seeing this remarkable animal had to wait for 10 years to see a rhinoceros. In 1810, a rhinoceros arrived at Portsmouth and was bought by Stephan Polito, the next owner of the Exeter Exchange menagerie. He exhibited the rhinoceros in his travelling menagerie and then at the Exeter Exchange. When Polito died in 1814, the rhinoceros was sold and taken to Rotterdam. It spent the next 10 years of its life touring Europe, and finally died of the cold in 1839.

whose arrival in London had touched my life with magic. Simply seeing the picture on that poster had changed so many things for me. Who knew what seeing the unicorn would do?

I remain, sir,
Your sincerely,
Susan Oldsmith

PS: Oh, sir, when will you bring a real live unicorn to London?

Strange but True

It was not only wild animals that were displayed in a menagerie. Sometimes, there were 'freak' animals, like a two-headed calf or a three-legged colt. There were human dwarves and giants. The stuffed bodies of unusual animals, or even their skeletons, also attracted large crowds.

Qs and As

How did the rhinoceros reach Pidcock's collection?

Interestingly, the rhinoceros was a present from the nawab of Lucknow in India for a nobleman in London. But the nawab had not bothered to find out if the rhinoceros was a welcome gift! As a result, when it reached London in June 1790, the owner sold it to Thomas Clark. It was finally bought by Gilbert Pidcock.

So, the rhinoceros lived for only three years after it arrived in England?

Yes, the rhinoceros died in 1793. It had stumbled and injured its foot several months ago. It was believed that this injury caused its death. Without proper medical attention or even knowledge about these creatures, it was difficult to say why they fell ill or died.

But Pidcock didn't really dig up the dead rhinoceros, did he?

Actually, he did. The rhinoceros died when the menagerie was travelling. By the time it reached Portsmouth, the body was smelling so badly that the city's mayor ordered that it be buried at once. Two weeks later, Pidcock went back to dig out the hide and bones of the rhinoceros.

A dead rhinoceros couldn't be worth anything, could it? Actually, it was worth a lot! Rhinoceros were not easy animals to trap. When angry, they could charge and cause a lot of harm. Even elephants are scared of them. Pidcock had probably spent a lot of money to buy the animal, feed and care for it. The death of the rhinoceros meant that he would not be able to earn this investment back. He wanted the hide and bones to stuff it because he was confident that people would flock to see the stuffed rhinoceros. Stuffing dead animals to display in their collection was something that every menagerie owner did.

Strange but True

Wombwell's travelling menagerie had an elephant that died. A rival menagerie, run by Atkins, gleefully put up a banner that announced that they had 'the only live elephant in the fair'. Wombwell put up a huge canvas that told the public that he had 'the only dead elephant at the fair.' Large crowds filled Wombwell's Menagerie, eager to see the dead elephant while Atkins's Menagerie was deserted.

The people of Europe were fascinated by rhinoceros. In 1749, a rhinoceros from Assam was sent to France. It became extremely popular, attracting huge crowds that came to see it. A dramatist whose play was being performed at the same time complained that the 'monster' was stealing his audience!

SECRET POST

A CRUEL VOYAGE ON THE SEAS

Animals were taken away from India not just for menageries, but also for 'pet' shops, such as Charles Jamrach's Radcliffe 'Wild-beast' shop, which was at the time reportedly the largest such shop in the world! Jamrach's business empire incuded a museum, the 'Jamrach's Animal Emporium' and a menagerie in London.

For all the animals being transported, the journey by sea meant storms and bad weather. How would the animals react to the pitching of the ship or the high waves slamming on the deck? In 1814, a rhinoceros was shipped from Calcutta. When the ship ran into a storm, the panic-stricken animal created havoc and the captain ordered it thrown overboard.

Animals were killed in accidents on the ship too. Or, sometimes, when the ship was becalmed, and food became scarce, the sailors had no option but to eat the animals they were responsible for transporting.

For an animal that managed to survive the harrowing journey and reach England, the English weather sometimes proved fatal. For instance, in 1799, Gilbert Pidcock bought a rhinoceros from India. However, it developed breathing difficulties a few months later and died.

Owners of menageries and keepers alike often knew very little about how to care for the animals. The rhinoceros that died in 1793 was regularly given wine to drink. It is believed that it stumbled because it was intoxicated and injured its foot, leading to its death months later. An elephant that arrived from India in 1720, died in just four months because it did not get sufficient or suitable food. This was primarily because of the ignorance of its keepers about its natural diet. Their lack of knowledge also led them to expose the animal to the cold.

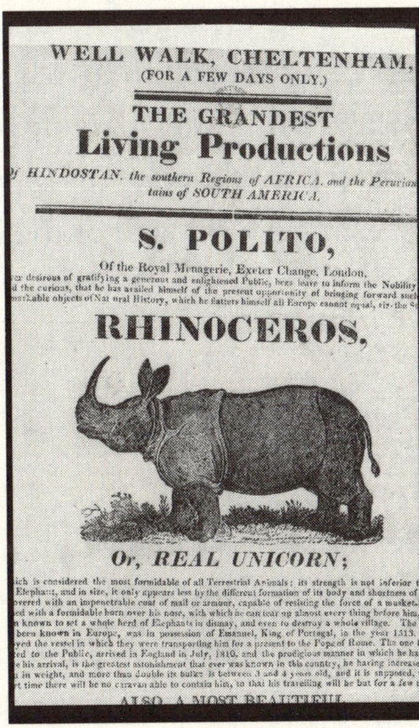

3

WHY WERE THEY NOT NAMED?

Names are important! And yet, the animals in the early menagerie collections were never named. Menagerie owners found creative ways to describe the animals, so the public would flock to see them. But when Pidcock's travelling menagerie stopped at a little village, a bunch of curious children who visited the animals, came away with questions for which they could find no answers. And so, they penned this charming letter to Mr Gilbert Pidcock of the Exeter Exchange menagerie.

24 April 1797

Dear Mr Pidcock,

Yesterday I visited your travelling menagerie with my sisters and brother. We hoped to see you because we had many questions we wanted to ask you. But you were away, and we were very disappointed. Who would tell us about the animals? Then Father bought a pamphlet about the menagerie and told us we had to share it. We didn't mind because the pamphlet gives us a lot of valuable and interesting information about the animals displayed in the menagerie.

But what about the people who cannot read? Or the people who do not want to spend money on a pamphlet? Such people, Father told us, talked to the keepers. These men not only knew things like what the animals ate, but also shared thrilling stories of how dangerous they could be.

We marvelled at the two-headed calf. Which head does it use when it needs to think? The Irish Dwarf amazed us

The people visiting the menagerie had only heard of tigers, rhinos and elephants. How would they learn more about these animals? Menagerie owners published pamphlets with information about the animals on display. These could be bought at the door and read as you walked past the exhibits. Stephen Polito, the next person to exhibit animals at the Exeter Exchange after Thomas Clark, published a book titled *Description and Natural History of S. Polito's Collection of Living Birds and Animals*, priced at one shilling.

When exotic wild animals were still very new in England, there was confusion about the actual names of the big cats. While lions were easy to identify, all other cats were called tigers. This often included leopards, panthers and cheetahs. One way of identifying the Indian tiger was by referring to it as the 'Royal' tiger.

because he was so small! Why, he was shorter than Tom and Theresa, and they are only six years old.

I liked the Royal tiger the best. How beautiful he was, with his fine stripes and the flash of gold. How his tail lashed from side to side! I wanted a tail like that, and my sister wanted to roar like the lioness we saw. And all Tom and Theresa would do was laugh.

They are twins and like to do the same things. So, when Theresa, who is the one with good ideas, said she was a laughing hyena, Tom immediately said he was too. They laughed so much that Father said they were Tom-hyena and Theresa-hyena.

At that, Theresa stopped laughing long enough to tell Father that Mr Pidcock's hyenas were not called Tom and Theresa. Naturally, Father wanted to know what they were called. None of us could remember. Theresa said the best way to find out was to visit Mr Pidcock's menagerie again. Tom immediately agreed with her. For a few moments it looked as if Father would have to take us again to see the animals.

Then he remembered that the menagerie had left the village that morning. None of us believed that. We had not heard the band playing or the people cheering.

Do you know which was one of the most beloved animals at the Exeter Exchange? It was a striped hyena! In 1821, a baby hyena arrived on a ship from India. He was meant for a geologist who wanted to carry out some experiments with the hyena's skull. Of course, this would have meant killing the hyena to get his skull! The hyena was a firm favourite with the sailors, who had named him Billy. When menagerie owner Edward Cross took delivery of the animal, he was struck by Billy's good temper. He begged for Billy's life and took him to the menagerie where the hyena charmed visitors and keepers alike for many years.

A band and music for a menagerie?

Why not? The arrival of a travelling menagerie was a great event in a town or village. The band marched ahead, playing lively music, followed by the animals. Large animals like elephants walked with their keepers by their side. Others, like a rhinoceros or a tiger, were safely stowed away in vans. A roar from a tiger or the shrill cry of a rhinoceros gave the villagers a glimpse of the treats awaiting them and made sure that they would come to see the animals.

Why, when the menagerie had come into the village, we had heard the music from far away. That's how we had all been waiting for it on the Main Street. And that's how we had managed to watch the parade.

Please, Mr Pidcock, could you play music even when your menagerie leaves town? That way, we can see the animals one more time and find out their names, too.

We spent the entire day guessing what the animals were called. Theresa came up with the silliest names and, of course, Tom had to think of even sillier ones. It was only much later that my sister Susan remembered something important. The animals in Pidcock's menagerie, she said, had no names. Not the laughing hyena, nor the gold-and-black-striped Indian tiger, and definitely not the wrinkly grey elephant that came from a deep jungle in India, according to the pamphlet.

We had all read the pamphlet several times. And so we knew that you had owned these animals for many years. Particularly the elephant, which had been with you for four years. How could you live with these animals and not name them? Why, we name every kitten, puppy, calf and chick as soon as it is born. All our pets know their names and come running when we call them. Even our youngest sister smiles when we call her name. And she is only a baby.

Your pamphlet said that the elephant had lived with its family in India. Surely, its mama must have named it. And the other elephants must have thought up other

The children were a little off the mark here because menagerie owners did not travel to India to find the animals for their collections. They simply bought them from sailors travelling on ships from India. In fact, there was such competition to get the rarest and most unusual animals that sometimes menagerie owners boarded a ship even before it had reached the docks. Some of these animals were displayed in their own menageries. Often, they sold the animals to other menageries.

names to tease it with. And yet, you could not think of a name for the elephant? What did you call it on the long journey from the jungle to the port in India? And on the ship to England...you must have talked to it, petted it, fed it. What did you call it then?

And now, when the elephant is far away from its family, surely you must talk to it as you put it into a caravan. When the elephant does its tricks and makes the people laugh, how do you praise it? Mr Pidcock, we are curious to know why you have not named the animals in your menagerie.

Is it because you could not think of names for these creatures? If that is the case, we are happy to help. We think Rajah is a good name for your elephant. Father says it means king. And there is nothing kinglier than an elephant. Most tigers, Father says, come from a place

Gilbert Pidcock was not the only menagerie owner who did not name his animals. Early accounts of the animals brought to England show that they were referred to simply as 'a young elephant', or 'a healthy rhinoceros'. Advertisements announcing a new elephant referred to it as 'scientific', 'stupendous' or a 'sagacious beast'. Over time, this attitude changed and the animals were named.

called Bengal in India. Isn't that a lovely name for your gold-striped Royal tiger?

We hope this will inspire you to think of names for the other animals in your collection. And the next time Pidcock's menagerie passes through our village, we hope to learn the names of all the animals in its show.

Menagerie owners could also buy animals from the wild animal dealers, who had contacts with suppliers and could provide any animal. Charles Jamrach was one of the best known of these dealers. Jamrach's shop was crammed with all kinds of animals, with no attempt made to keep them comfortable, if nothing else. They were all in small cages, stacked on top of each other. Often, you would find a carnivore right next to its prey. Animals and birds died of stress and ill-health caused by the terrible living conditions.

If you need any help naming your animals, please do not hesitate to contact us.

We remain,

Yours faithfully,

Charles Mason, Susan Mason, Theresa Mason, Tom Mason and Baby Grace Mason

Qs and As

So, what was the story behind the elephant that was with Gilbert Pidcock for many years?

Sadly, details of where the elephant had lived and how it had been trapped were rarely considered important enough to be recorded. The elephant's story began from the moment it was taken on board an East Indiaman (this was what ships sailing from major European countries to ports in India were called) named *Rose*. The ship reached England in 1793, and the elephant was at some point purchased by Gilbert Pidcock. It was with him for nine years and died, nameless, in 1802.

Why was it not named?

There is no explanation offered for not naming the animals that earned the menagerie owners a lot of money and brought them great fame. After all, it was the animals who helped their owners get an invitation to the homes of lords, dukes and even the king of the country. Despite this, the animals were treated only as money-generating machines. So, they were kept healthy to protect the money invested in them. But there was no attempt to know them beyond this. Not one of the three rhinoceros that were brought to England during this time, was named.

This worked to the menagerie owner's advantage because one elephant could be replaced by another without the visitors ever finding out.

Why did the owners not spend money to care for the animals, since they earned from them?

The menagerie owners expected the animals to be on show all the time. Owners of the menageries and many keepers alike were ignorant about the wants and needs of the animals, resulting in frequent deaths of animals. As the number of animal deaths mounted, menagerie owners began to insure the animals, to protect their investments. Gilbert Pidcock insured the elephant for 750 pounds. In 1867, the straw in the giraffe house in the London Zoo caught fire at night. Two giraffes died in the fire. The Sun Fire Insurance Office paid 545 pounds as compensation. This was probably the first claim of this kind to be paid in Europe.

Strange but True

In 1850, an old lady at a menagerie stood outside the elephant's stall, waiting for the animal to turn so she could see its head. You see, she thought the trunk was the tail! A man, watching a parade, thought the elephant was walking backwards because the trunk looked like a tail!

Still More Letters

Look, here are more letters addressed to Mr Pidcock. Let's see who has been writing to him!

Dear Sir,

I am the captain of the East Indiaman *Tulip*, a ship recently returned from India. I have two animals that might be of interest to you. One is a young Bengal tiger in the prime of health. It has been fed fresh meat on the journey and has consumed more than 15 goats. The other is a young elephant, about two years of age. If you are interested in purchasing these animals, please contact me at the dock, where the *Tulip* is berthed.

Yours sincerely,

Captain Jones

Dear Mr Pidcock,

Last week I purchased some animals from you. They were delivered to me today. Upon opening the box, I found that the leopard and two monkeys were dead. What am I to do with them? Kindly return the amount paid for these. If you fail to do so, I will be forced to go to court.

Yours faithfully,

Abraham Saunders

Dear Sir,
Since I have recently come home from a voyage to India, I have two boas in my possession. These lived in Madras and were captured by me. They are in good condition and are active and lively. I am willing to sell them for a sum of £10.

Yours faithfully,
James Burton

Dear Mr Pidcock,
This is to inform you of the misfortune that struck us last night.

Soon after you set out for London, there was a terrible thunderstorm. The lightning frightened the horses very much indeed and they ran away, dragging the van behind them. The van was overturned and the two ostriches in it were killed.

Yours faithfully,
David White

Dear Mr Pidcock,
I write to you from the Tower of London. Last week you left a large cat with us, to be collected soon. This morning, it escaped. When the keeper, Mr Mason, tried to capture it, the cat leapt on him and injured him. I regret to inform you that we had to shoot the animal dead. Mr Mason is recovering slowly but steadily.

Yours faithfully,
Keeper of the Tower

4

WHO CLIPS THE LION'S NAILS?

Clipping nails and cutting hair are things we take for granted. We do them regularly and they help us stay clean and healthy. Lions and tigers in the wild too have a system to groom themselves. But what happens when they are taken out of their habitats and put into small cages with wooden floors and iron bars?

Let's take a peep into the Exeter Exchange menagerie, now run by Stephen Polito, who owned a travelling menagerie too. That meant Mr Polito had good experience with animals. But did that mean that he could answer this very important question posed by a curious child?

10 November 1813

Dear Mr Polito,

Yesterday was my birthday. I had cake, of course, and gifts. The best gift came from Uncle Robert, who knows well what I like. Do you know what his gift was? He took me to see the wild animals at the Exeter Exchange menagerie!

Most children were taken to see the animals at the Exeter Exchange menagerie. A visit here was considered educational and made in the hope that the young visitors would learn something about the animals displayed there.

This was something that I had long wanted to do. Because, you see, I had never seen the animals there. I had heard them, though, when we drove past the building. Such loud noises of roaring, snarling and growling sounded that my sister called the building the Growl Menagerie! Why, the noise once scared our horse as we drove past. And forgetting the carriage with Mama, my little sister Ruby and me in it, off he ran! How we were bumped and jolted and shaken in the carriage. Mama was very annoyed. She said the animals in the menagerie were too wild to be seen by little children. Ruby and I were very disappointed and knew we would have to wait to see the wild beasts.

I am 10 now and even Mama had to admit that I was almost grown up. And that's why she allowed me to go with Uncle. Poor Ruby is only eight years old and so she

People walking or riding past the Exeter Exchange building were often disturbed by the noises made by the animals. They wrote letters to the newspapers, complaining about the disturbance caused by the roars and screams of animals. There were pleas to move the menagerie away from the heart of the city. When the animals were particularly restless, the road outside the menagerie was cordoned off.

had to stay home. But I promised to tell her everything that I saw at the menagerie.

That's why I looked carefully at every little thing, reminding myself that Ruby was waiting to hear about the smallest detail about the menagerie. I looked at the large pictures painted on the building. I stared at the men calling out to passers-by, telling them about all the wonderful animals they would see inside. There were birds, bright and loud, adding their voices to the calls of the men. Then, I found myself in a dark and gloomy place, with small stalls lining the sides. There was a crowd of people here, shopping for things.

We left them to their shopping, Uncle Robert and I, and walked up the stairs to the first floor. The murmur of people's voices died away and now the noise of the animals grew louder. And the smell! How could I describe it to Ruby? It was thick and wild and sour. It smelt of things that were rotting, and under that was the green smell of leaves and sap. Would Ruby understand exactly what I meant, I worried as we walked up. Then we walked into the menagerie and I forgot everything in the wonder of seeing the wild animals.

I saw a large hall, with cages lined on one side. On the other side were birds tied to perches, smaller animals chained to little stands and bright-eyed monkeys crowded in cages. There were ladies, holding up their fine dresses so that they wouldn't touch the floor, children peering into the cages and men talking loudly about the animals.

The menagerie attracted all kinds of people. We already know that the members of the royal family were keenly interested in exotic animals. Dr Joshua Brookes, surgeon and anatomist, was a regular visitor and dissected several of the menagerie animals. The most famous of these was Chunee (or Chuny), whom you will meet soon. Artists like Thomas and his brother Edwin Landseer visited the menagerie too, to observe the animals and sketch them. Edwin Landseer went on to become one of the most famous animal painters of the time, and also sculpted the lions that are a part of Nelson's Column in Trafalgar Square.

I was so busy looking around that I never noticed who pushed me. Before I knew what was happening, I found myself stumbling backwards, falling hard on the display of animals. These animals were not in cages. Some of them were chained to little tables or on perches. The birds flapped excitedly and screeched in my ears, and a small animal hissed at my feet, leaping at the end of its chain. The monkeys jumped and screamed and stretched out greedy paws, ready to grab anything in their reach. I felt their fingers in my hair and had a moment of panic. Then Uncle Robert grabbed my hand and tugged me away. It was not an experience I wanted to remember, but I had promised to tell Ruby everything, hadn't I?

Accidents were common in the menagerie. One side of the hall was taken up with cages for the large animals. On the other side were displays of birds and smaller animals. This left only a narrow passage for the visitors to walk. On days when the hall was crowded, people were sometimes pushed on to the animals, resulting in injuries.

A keeper pushed through the crowd and came at once to check if I was all right. Uncle Robert spoke angrily to him about the crowd in the hall. What could the keeper say? He nodded and agreed that people were thoughtless and forgot their manners when they came to the menagerie. I could see that he wanted to tell us stories about how badly behaved the visitors could be. But Uncle Robert wasn't interested and asked instead about the big cats. I was disappointed because I am sure the keeper knew many tales. Then I saw the lion and forgot the crowds, the noise, the smell, and even my recent fright.

The lion…it was a creature of gold. The Royal tiger was muscled silk, padding endlessly from one end of its cage to the other. The keeper told us that the tiger

Imagine wanting to watch someone eat their dinner! Sounds strange, doesn't it? But the sight of the wild animals feeding was a great attraction. The people of England were eager to see the 'fierce' nature of the wild animals, but stuffed into small cages with barely enough room to move, the lions and tigers could do nothing but roar. Feeding time was an opportunity to see them at their wildest. The animals were not fed on Sunday so that they would be ravenous on Monday. Visitors to the menagerie on Monday could therefore enjoy a 'savage' show. At some point in the history of the menagerie, visitors had to pay extra to watch the animals being fed.

had been captured in the jungles of India. I looked at the tiger and wondered what it thought of the people crowding to see it, or their loud voices and gasps of admiration. Just then the elephant at the end of the hall rang a little bell and the noise in the hall grew louder. It was time to feed the animals, the keeper told us.

Other men appeared, carrying buckets and pans. They poured birdseed into the bowls for the birds that were tied to perches, and hay for the elephant. But all eyes were fixed on the lion and the tigers. Large slabs of meat, red and dripping, were thrown into their cages. The animals snarled as they leapt on it. They growled at anyone who dared to move any closer to their cages.

Interestingly, several years later, the people of London objected to the sight of snakes being fed rabbits! Angry letters were written to the newspapers and the zoo authorities had to ensure that the reptile house was closed to visitors during the snakes' feeding time.

They shook the meat and then tore into it, claws ripping and teeth tearing.

People murmured and whispered in awe. The hall filled with the sound of bones crunching and loud chewing.

Animals, I told Uncle Robert, didn't have to mind their manners or do the things humans had to. They could eat with their mouths open and no one would scold them for it. Why, I said, they did not even need to worry about clipping their nails. The keeper heard me and told me I was wrong. The lion and tigers did have their nails clipped. I stared at him. Was he teasing me? Surely no one would have the courage to go into a lion's or tiger's cage!

The keeper saw that I didn't believe him and so, he told us how it was done. First, he said, the animal's paws were tied. The keepers used straps with slip knots to grab the paws. This was useful in pulling the animals close to the bars of the cage. That was when one of the keepers cut the animal's nails.

> The wild animals in cages could not scratch and scrape against tree bark or other natural surfaces to keep their nails in check. Sometimes, these grew so long that they were embedded in the soft pads of their claws. When this happened, the animal suffered great pain and walked with a limp.

A crowd had gathered around us and everyone was listening to the keeper. I could see that many of them didn't believe the keeper's story. I was not very sure that it was so easy to cut a tiger's or lion's nails. What if the beast tried to reach through the bars and bite the man, someone wondered.

The keeper allowed himself a small smile, as if amused at this idea. The big danger, he said, was if the animal tried to bite the bars of the cage. It would end up with broken teeth and not be able to eat meat. So, a second keeper stood with a block of wood at the end of a long

When big animals were transported from India, they came with their own Indian keepers to take care of them. The elephants had their mahout, who stayed a few months to settle the animal in the new country before returning to India. Most of these men were very attached to their animals and found it difficult to part from them. In 1800, when a few cheetahs were brought over from the collection of Tipu Sultan, the ruler of Mysuru who had been defeated by the British army, three Indian keepers accompanied them. When it was time to return to India, they wept at having to part from their favourite beasts. Sadly, there is no record of where these keepers were from and what their names were.

stick. This was pushed in front of the animal's mouth, so it would not harm itself by biting the bars. There was a whoosh of relief from the crowd and I saw that several were smiling. They all agreed that it was a good idea and congratulated the keeper.

What about the tigers that live in the jungles of India, I asked the keeper. Who cut their nails in the forests? There was a sudden burst of laughter and I saw that many people were smiling at my question. But the keeper didn't laugh. No one, he told me. In the jungles, the lions and tigers slashed at trees and rubbed their paws to keep their nails short and sharp. I thought that was wonderful.

My sister Ruby did not. She frowned horribly and then asked if there were trees in the menagerie. I stared at her. Hadn't she heard a word I had just said? How could there be trees on the first and second floors of a

The people who ran the zoos and menageries often interfered cruelly in the lives of the animals. When the first hippopotamus was born in the London Zoo, instead of letting the mother take care of it, the authorities decided to raise the baby hippopotamus. The baby died, and so did the next one they tried to raise. The third baby, which the mother was allowed to feed and raise, survived.

building? Besides, there was no room in the cages for a tree to grow. There was barely space for the animals to lie down and stretch out. There was nothing in the cage except the floor and the bars.

At that, Ruby jumped to her feet shouting that it was wicked and mean to keep tigers like this.

Very few people spared a thought for the animals or worried about how to keep them comfortable and healthy. The general idea was that these animals were better off in England, in clean cages and with good food given to them, than in India. It was only much later, in 1855, that a letter sent to a newspaper demanded, 'Why do we coop these noble animals in such nutshells of cages? What a miserable sight to see them pace backwards and forwards in their box-like dens!'

I thought of the keepers who looked after the animals and made sure they were fed on time every day. But Ruby only shook her head and said it didn't matter. So I reminded her about the keepers who kept the animals healthy and even clipped their nails.

Exactly, Ruby said. And then she asked me a question. And though I am two years older than her and I have seen the menagerie and she has not, I did not know the answer. Nor did Father or Mother. And Ruby needs an answer to her question. So, Father suggested that I write to you and ask you the question.

Will you please tell me, Mr Polito, why can't the lions and tigers have real trees in their cages to sharpen their claws?

Waiting eagerly for your reply,
I remain,
Yours faithfully,
Clara Turnbull

Ruby was right to say that being fed on time was not the most important thing. The lions and tigers, used to hunting in the wild, were forced to eat the meat that the keepers gave them. Even if it was the freshest meat, it still came from a dead animal. Also, this meant that the animals did not get the exercise they needed to stay fit. The feeding time was fixed to suit the visitors, not the animals. In 1823, the feeding time of the big cats was changed from 9 p.m. to 8 p.m. to suit the children who visited the menagerie.

Qs and As

Why were the animals kept in such small cages?

The primary reason was that the people of England knew very little about these animals. To them, they represented the exotic wilderness of India, which they were eager to explore. But since they could not think of making the long journey to India, they satisfied themselves by looking at the animals. The focus was on evoking a feeling of awe and fear in the visitors. But no thought was given to how the animals had lived in India, or what would suit them best in a strange new country. This was the reason for the small, bare cages with hard floors and no space for the animals to move.

So, why did the lions and tigers roar so loudly?

Imagine being put into a tiny cage and kept there for years. The animals had no exercise since there was barely any room to walk. The menagerie was open from 9 a.m. to 9 p.m. every day from Monday to Saturday. During these hours, there was a constant stream of visitors walking up and down past the cages of the animals. In addition to the chatter and laughter, there were always people who liked to throw things at the animals, and poke and prod them.

Strange but True

A young boy was a regular visitor to the menagerie at the Exeter Exchange. The owner, Edward Cross, often gave him dead animals to dissect. The boy honed his dissection skills on these and was soon well known for his skill in stuffing dead animals. This was Abraham Dee Bartlett, who went on to become the director of the Regent's Zoo Park.

SECRET POST

THE MENAGERIE KEEPER'S WORK

Keepers were the most important people in the life of a menagerie animal. They cleaned out the cages and took care of the animals. They were often the first to notice any signs of ill-health in the animals and nurse them back to health. When Regent's Park Zoo got Jumbo the elephant from a zoo in France, the animal was dirty, with injuries all over his body. Jumbo was handed over to a keeper who cared for him until he was healthy again. The bond between the keeper and the elephant was so strong that Jumbo would listen to no one else. When Regent's Park Zoo sold Jumbo to a circus in the USA, Jumbo refused to step out of his enclosure. Finally, the keeper was offered the job of taking care of the elephant. Jumbo listened to the keeper and travelled to the USA with him. And the keeper stayed with Jumbo and took good care of him.

Being a keeper could be dangerous too. The temper of the caged animals was uncertain and, sometimes, a keeper who stepped into the enclosure was injured badly. Despite the risks involved in being a keeper and the kind of work these people did, the keepers remained largely unnamed and unappreciated.

The Menagerie in the Tower

Inside the menagerie
at the Exeter Exchange

5

DO ELEPHANTS STOP GROWING?

Chunee was the most famous elephant in the history of the Exeter Exchange menagerie. When Chunee was first bought by Edward Cross, the owner of the menagerie after Stephen Polito's death, he was not named. He was referred to as 'a young male elephant' or 'an Asian elephant'. Chunee was the biggest attraction of the menagerie and most people were happy to marvel at his size and his weight. Except for this young girl, who wondered how Chunee put up with being a prisoner.

27 December 1811

Dear Chunee,

You don't know me, but I know all about you. My sister saw you on the stage at Covent Garden yesterday. She said the pantomime *Harlequin and Padmanaba, or*

An animal on stage? Why would anyone do that? But they did. Two other theatres had introduced animals on the stage. Dogs were included in a performance at the Sadler's Wells Theatre and horses at the Drury Lane Theatre in London. Naturally, it was felt necessary for the theatre at Covent Garden to do something similar, so an elephant was introduced on the stage for the first time.

The Golden Fish was the best she had ever seen. I have never seen a pantomime or an elephant, leave alone an elephant in a pantomime.

It is because I am only seven years old. And Mama says little girls of seven don't go to watch pantomimes.

Do little girls of eight watch pantomimes?

Your friend,

Charlotte

1 January 1812

Dear Chunee,

I have heard so many stories about you. My sister says your home is in India. I don't know anything about

India, except that it is very far away. And that it is very hot there. You have lived in hot India. And now you live in cool England. It must be wonderful to travel to new places. I have never been anywhere. I have always lived in our house in London.

My sister has talked of nothing but the pantomime! She even acts out little bits of it. She showed me how regally you walked on to the stage and how gently you knelt down. And she told me how excited everyone got when they saw you. They shouted, she said, and several of them clapped hard. Didn't that frighten Chunee, I wondered, and my sister looked surprised. She said she had not thought about such a big elephant being frightened.

For the audience of the time, an elephant was something new and exciting. And of course, seeing it on the stage was even more of a novelty. However, very few of them understood that this was a wild animal and could, therefore, be dangerous. As late as 1863, a man named James Turner brought five young lions to a dinner he hosted for his friends. Not one of the people at the party wondered if it was right to pet wild animals in this manner. Instead, everyone had a grand time playing with them.

Do small things frighten big elephants…and little girls too?

Your friend,

Charlotte

Charlotte was right to wonder if the noise frightened Chunee. Imagine an animal used to the freedom of a jungle, being forced to go into a building, and then pushed in front of a noisy crowd. Chunee was certainly startled by the noise and rushed away from it as soon as he could.

Chunee was not very comfortable onstage. It is possible that the manager realized it could be dangerous and let the elephant go. But Chunee's acting career was not yet over because he went on to perform at Astley's Theatre. Here, he was a part of a large procession that included horses and many people. After several of these performances, Chunee was finally taken to the Exeter Exchange menagerie.

4 February 1812
Dear Chunee,
I have been trying to grow as fast as I can. Then, I will be allowed to go to the pantomime and see you. But my sister says you are no longer at Covent Garden. You have retired from stage, she says.

I have a question for you, though: Do elephants retire?

Your friend,

Charlotte

No animal that could be used to earn money for its owner was ever allowed to retire. Remember how the rhinoceros that had hurt its leg in 1792 continued to be exhibited even though it was unwell. Menagerie owners rarely allowed the ill-health of animals to come in the way of making money.

10 July 1812
Dear Chunee,
I just heard that you have moved to the Exeter Exchange menagerie. That's three places you have been to in England. You have seen the docks of London, Covent

Garden and now the menagerie. And I have not even been to two of these.

Do you dream of going to more new places?

Your friend,

Charlotte

> For an animal, travelling was never a pleasant experience. For smaller animals it meant being crammed into cramped cages that were loaded into vans. For a large animal like an elephant, it usually meant walking long distances.

11 September 1814

Dear Chunee,

Mama says if I am good and don't bother her with too many questions, Papa will take me to the Exeter Exchange menagerie.

How many questions does it take to become too many questions?

Your friend,

Charlotte

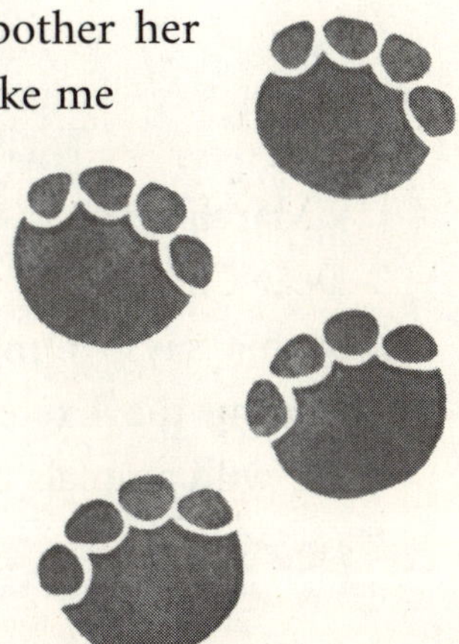

27 December 1815

Dear Chunee,

I finally saw you yesterday.

Did you see me?

Your friend,

Charlotte

4 June 1816

Dear Chunee,

Everyone says I am tall for a 12-year-old. But when I saw you, I knew how little I was.

I am as high as Mama's shoulder, but I had to tip my head up to look at you.

Do you tip your head up to look at anyone?

Your friend,

Charlotte

7 March 1818

Dear Chunee,

Mama says young ladies should not be interested in visiting the Exeter Exchange menagerie or talk about the wild animals there. She must be talking about some other young lady because I don't look at the wild animals. I only look at you.

> The display of animals in the Exeter Exchange was constantly changing. Animals died or were sold, and new animals were added to the collection. During the years that Chunee was at the menagerie, it certainly had a lion, a tiger, a llama, a leopard, a panther, a jaguar, two sloth bears, a camel from Egypt, different kinds of monkeys and birds, kangaroos and emus.

You are bigger than I remember you from two years ago.

> Charlotte was right. Chunee was bigger. Remember that he came to England as a six-year-old. He must have been around 12 or 13 years old at this time. He was certainly still growing and had not attained his final height or weight.

It seems to me that you wear your cage like a well-fitting dress. When I grow a little, Mama sighs and looks annoyed. But then she gets one of the maids to open up my dresses. Then I can breathe and move easily in my clothes.

Will your cage be let out too, so you have room to breathe and move in it?

Your friend,

Charlotte

> Yes, Chunee's cage was widened at some point to make room for him. But in the cramped menagerie at the Exeter Exchange, how large could the cage be made? It could never be big enough for an animal like Chunee to be comfortable. Besides, remember that the elephant had still not finished growing. This meant that in a very short time, Chunee's cell was once again too small for him.

20 September 1818

Dear Chunee,

I have grown again and Mama is not happy. She sighed and clicked her tongue and said I should not eat so much butter. She said it was time I stopped growing. How can I stop myself growing?

A newspaper reports that you are now nearly 10 feet tall and weigh over 4 tonnes. That means you are still growing.

When do elephants stop growing?

Your friend,

Charlotte

Chunee was the largest animal ever seen in Europe. He is reported to have been nearly 11 feet tall and weighing 5 tonnes, and was called 'the animated mountain'.

9 June 1820

Dear Chunee,

Mama tried to tempt me with a visit to the theatre for my birthday. But I wanted to see you. There have been stories about you in the newspaper – about your bad temper and how you smashed things in anger. People say that you cannot be trusted, that you are dangerous. I know that feeling of being shut in, of seeing walls wherever I turn. When I feel that way, I am afraid that I will forget all the things that Mama has taught me and scream at someone. I escape to the garden then. A little brisk walking there and I feel calmer. You need to go out, too. After all, you must have walked in the jungles of India.

Why don't they let you walk here?

Your friend,

Charlotte

Charlotte was right. What Chunee needed was exercise. Instead, his bad temper was treated with medicines. Naturally, these did not in any way improve his temper or change his behaviour. Instead, he became suspicious of food, and the people around him.

18 August 1823

Dear Chunee,

I saw you yesterday. But you didn't look like the Chunee of old. Your eyes were small and angry, and you trumpeted again and again in rage. I could see that your behaviour scared people.

They murmured anxiously and backed nervously away every time you moved. They were glad of the keepers who poked you cruelly to get you to behave.

The keepers were provided with long sticks with sharp ends to control the elephant, not understanding that this only annoyed him further. When Chunee became very restless, his tusks were cut off. Perhaps this was done to ensure that the elephant did not injure himself, but it was still a brutal way to get Chunee to 'behave'.

They don't understand that all you want is to step out of your cage, to go down the steps of the menagerie and be free. They don't believe that elephants and curious girls need to be free. They can't imagine how trapped you feel, living within the same walls and doing the same things every day. But I can.

It must certainly have been horrible for Chunee, to be trapped in a small cage with no space to move or even lie down comfortably. Edward Cross tried to sell Chunee and was relieved to find an American willing to pay 500 pounds for him. Perhaps Chunee's new home might have had more room for him. But there was no ship available at that time to transport such a huge animal and the sale fell through.

And that's why I am glad, glad, *glad* to be escaping. I am finally going away, Chunee, leaving London for new horizons. I am getting married. It may be that I have exchanged my old cage for a new one. But at least it will not be the cage I have seen all my life, and that gives me hope and allows me to dream of happiness. Then I look at you, and I see the same hunger in you.

Oh, Chunee, when will you step out of your cage and be free?

Your friend,

Charlotte

Qs and As

Who was Chunee?

In July 1811, a male elephant arrived on board the East Indiaman *Astel*. This elephant was around six years old at this time. He was bought by the manager of the Covent Garden theatre for 800 pounds. Six Indian seamen were hired to take care of the elephant and to train him. After a short career on the stage, Chunee was moved to the Exeter Exchange. He walked up the ramp to the first floor of the Exeter Exchange menagerie sometime in 1812. And he spent the next 14 years there.

So, what exactly did Chunee do at the menagerie?

Chunee was taught tricks and he showed off those tricks to the people who came to the menagerie. When asked how many men or women there were in the room, Chunee was able to give the right answer! Do you know how he did this? He huffed out the answer! So, if there were four men, Chunee would let out four short breaths. If asked how many women there were, he would similarly huff to give the right answer! He astonished the visitors by stealing money from the pockets of the men and charmed them by returning it.

It sounds like Chunee was an even-tempered animal. Why did he begin to misbehave then?

Chunee was a young elephant when he came to the menagerie in 1812. Over the next few years, he grew older and bigger, but there was no change in the routine he followed, nothing new to excite him. This lack of exercise annoyed him and he began to express his rage by ramming the bars of his cage. The carpenter was too frightened to try to repair the damaged bars. The menagerie workers were worried. What if Chunee managed to break out and broke down the other cages too? The other fear was that the floor would collapse beneath Chunee's immense weight and fall on the people shopping in the market below. This was when Edward Cross, the owner of the menagerie, decided that Chunee would have to be killed.

How did the people react to Chunee's death?

Chunee was the most famous animal in the menagerie and people were shocked by his death. Letters and poems mourning his death appeared in the newspapers. 'Farewell, poor Chuny! Generous beast, farewell!' one of the poems began. A play titled *Chuneelah: Or the Death of the Elephant at Exeter Change* was performed in the city. Edward Cross displayed Chunee's dead body at the menagerie, charging people a shilling each to view it. Large crowds came to see the dead animal. Finally, the stink from the decomposing body was so bad that Edward Cross was ordered to get rid of it. A dozen butchers worked for hours to get the skin off the body before cutting it up. Edward Cross displayed Chunee's skeleton to many visitors. There were rumours that Chunee had been suffering from a toothache and that was the reason for his angry behaviour.

Strange but True

Chunee was the not the only animal killed in a menagerie. In the Liverpool Zoological Garden, an elephant named Rajah trampled on his keeper and killed him in 1848. Rajah too, like Chunee, was kept in a cell inside a building. Rajah had disobeyed his keeper. As a result, the keeper had punished him by beating him with a broom. Annoyed by the beating, Rajah had knocked the keeper over. The owner of the zoo decided that the elephant was too dangerous to be kept and tried to feed him a poisoned bun. Rajah refused to eat the bun and the owner called in the soldiers who shot the animal dead.

SECRET POST

ALL THE NEWS ABOUT CHUNEE

If you lived in London in the nineteenth century, this is what you could expect to read in the newspaper from 27 February 1826 to 2 March 1826.

27 FEBRUARY 1826: CHUNEE RESTLESS

People walking or driving down the Strand yesterday were startled at the loud noises coming from the Exeter Exchange menagerie. The people of the area have for long been used to the roars and growls of animals, but yesterday several shoppers in the building were frightened out of their wits.

It was revealed that Chunee, the Indian elephant at the menagerie, was in a bad temper. He battered at the cage in a rage, damaging the thick walls. No carpenter was willing to do the repairs. It can only be hoped that Chunee will be soothed by the love of his keepers.

28 FEBRUARY 1826: CHUNEE CANNOT BE SOOTHED

The latest news about the largest animal in Europe is not good. Chunee's anger shows no signs of abating. The Indian elephant, usually one of the gentlest animals in the menagerie, refuses to let his keepers come anywhere near him. Any attempt to reach in through the bars of the cage infuriates him. Chunee has already tried to attack his keepers several times.

The elephant's fury has distressed the other animals in the menagerie, who also add their troubled cries to the fearful trumpeting of the beast. The broken bars of Chunee's cage have still not been repaired. There is growing fear that if Chunee happens to escape, he will easily destroy the cages of the other animals and set them free.

SECRET POST

1 MARCH 1826: WILL THE ROOF FALL?

The shopping area in the Exeter Exchange building has been deserted for the past two days. Now the entire section of the Strand has been cordoned off at both ends, and guards placed there. The reason is the behaviour of Chunee, the elephant in the menagerie.

Chunee, who weighs nearly 5 tonnes, has been in a bad temper for the past few days. The menagerie staff are now worried about what his constant stamping might be doing to the floor of the cage. Although the floor was strengthened before moving Chunee in, the keepers are afraid that it may give way under Chunee's stomping feet.

2 MARCH 1826: CHUNEE, BELOVED OF THOUSANDS, IS NO MORE

As Chunee was showing no signs of calming down, Mr Cross, the owner of the menagerie, arrived at a difficult decision — the elephant would have to be killed. However, the first attempt to kill him, by giving the animal poison, failed. Chunee, having smelt the poison in the hay, refused to eat it. How could the 11-foot-tall elephant weighing 5 tonnes be killed inside the menagerie?

That was when firearms were fetched and attempts made to shoot down Chunee. But this only angered the elephant even more and he tried to attack the men trying to kill him.

That was when Mr Cross called for the soldiers. A band of them reached the menagerie to find it shaking under the impact of the elephant's angry runs. The large room echoed with the screams of the animals and for a time it seemed as if the building would collapse. Then the soldiers began to fire at Chunee, and the noise rose. As many as 150 musket balls were fired at the beast, but nothing would stop him. He screamed still and raced for the bars, ramming them heavily with his head. It seemed as if the elephant was indestructible and people feared he would burst out of his cage very soon.

It was at that moment that a keeper thrust a sharp spear into the elephant. Chunee screamed as blood gushed out of the wound. Then, he slowly sank to his knees. For a moment, his great flanks heaved. Then, he let out a long breath, and did not breathe again. Thus ended

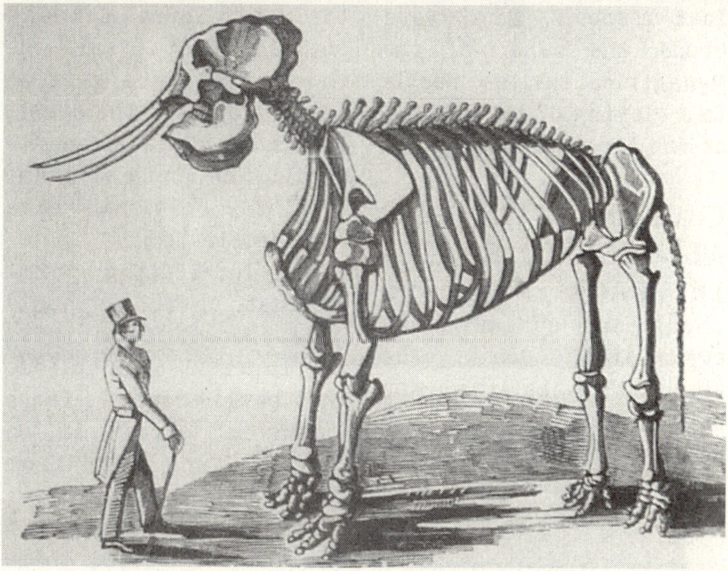

ABOVE: Chunee's skeleton on display; RIGHT: An advertisement about Chunee's hide

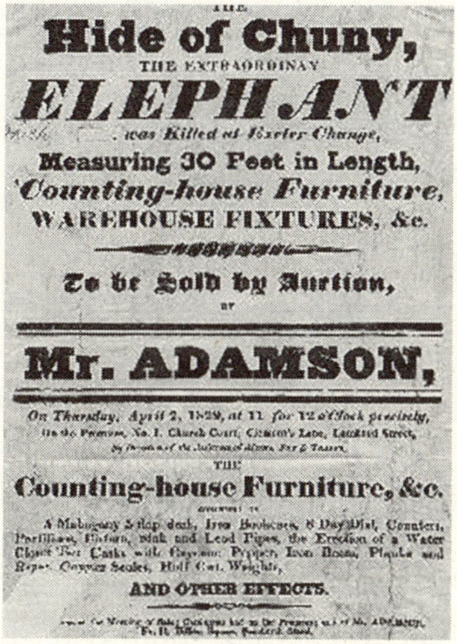

the life of the largest animal in Europe, the elephant that everyone knew as Chunee.

3 MARCH 1826: HAVE YOU SEEN CHUNEE YET?

For all those who loved the gentle Chunee, here is an opportunity to pay your last respects. Mr Edward Cross, the owner of the Menagerie, invites people to a viewing of the carcass of the large animal.

CHUNEE, STILL NOT ALLOWED TO REST IN PEACE

Chunee was not left alone even after death. The elephant's skeleton was put on display and his hide was auctioned by a company called Counting-house Furniture.

NEWS OF OTHER ELEPHANTS

King George III married Princess Charlotte in 1761. What do you think the new queen received as a late wedding gift? In 1763, she was given two elephants that had come from India!

In 1764, the queen was gifted two more elephants, one in May and the other in July.

The queen received her fifth elephant in 1763, from Bombay. And when an important official of the East India Company retired that year, he chose to bring a gift of an elephant for the queen. That made it six elephants in all. The sixth elephant lived for only two years and died in 1775.

An interesting thing is that these elephants were brought from India to impress and please the royal couple. These elephants lived in a country far away from their homes without ever being named. It was as if they had fulfilled their purpose once they had been given to the queen, and no further interest was necessary.

Perhaps this had something to do with the fact that the queen's elephants were not seen by the general public. Just over 60 years later, the situation had changed considerably. The Regent's Park Zoo owned an elephant named Jumbo, who was sold to an American circus owner named P.T. Barnum. The news created a huge uproar in England, with children writing letters to the newspapers and the zoo, begging for Jumbo to be allowed to stay on. Large crowds came to the zoo, to see Jumbo the elephant one last time. The visitors brought Jumbo cakes and pastries, fruits, biscuits and sweets. But it made no difference to the owner and Jumbo sailed away in a ship to join the circus.

Jumbo just did not want to leave the zoo, and the nation's heart went out to him.

6

IS IT THE ELEPHANT'S FAULT?

When Chunee the Indian elephant killed his keeper, all of London was both shocked and dismayed. Had Chunee gone rogue? And then the coroner handling the case, who was about to pronounce judgement on the elephant, received a letter from the hunter who had trapped Chunee in the jungles of India.

Capturing wild elephants in India was a difficult and a dangerous task. Once the elephant was captured, it had to be transported to the nearest port and then put on a ship to England. The people who helped capture and tame these animals never knew what happened to them once they sailed away. What if they learnt that an elephant they had sent to England had killed a man there? What would the British hunter, who had captured the animal, and the Indians who had worked with him, think?

2 November 1825
Dear Mr Coroner,
The contents of this letter are sure to surprise you. But ever since the news about the elephant Chunee reached me, I have been in shock.

> In a 'shocking' incident, Chunee, the elephant in the Exeter Exchange menagerie, had killed his keeper, John Tietjen.

Chunee, you see, was one of the elephants that I trapped. I do not remember the elephant or how he behaved when he was caught by my team. But I have spent the last 10 years here, in a village called Kumbha, and I have learnt a lot about the people and their animals.

Kumbha is a small village, made up of a handful of huts. Every resident of Kumbha is trained in the art of dealing with elephants. People say it is a skill passed on from fathers to sons and mothers to daughters. But I believe it is more than that. The people of Kumbha have a connection with elephants. They understand them and they know how to treat them.

I have often felt that our people in England lack this understanding of the animals. And every time I send

Do you know how elephants were trapped? There were three methods and the most popular one was called *keddah*. This involved building a fence around a herd of elephants. Fires were lit around the fence and the animals driven into an enclosure. In the second method, single male elephants were lured by tame female elephants. Sometimes, pits were dug and the elephants were trapped when they fell into these.

The *keddah* method of catching elephants was developed only in the 1870s by a British naturalist G.P. Sanderson, who worked in the public works department of Mysore (now Mysuru), to capture elephants who destroyed crop fields. So, Chunee was probably trapped by another method.

elephants or tigers back home, I hope they meet a keeper who will take good care of them.

Here, among the people of Kumbha, I have seen a very different attitude to animals. So I would like you to hear what they have to say about Chunee. It may be that in the time taken for this letter to travel across the seas, you will already have tried and punished Chunee. But there will be other elephants, trapped in the forests of Kumbha and sent to England. And I hope this will help you understand the animals, and what it is they need.

Ghasee Ram, the Village Headman

'We have heard of Chunee the elephant's behaviour and we are deeply ashamed of him. An elephant of Kumbha has killed a man. In our eyes, the elephant is a criminal and deserves to be punished.'

People were shocked when they heard that Chunee had killed John Tietjen. There were demands for him to be punished and that is why the coroner was called in to examine the case and give the verdict.

Tara Bai, the Wise Woman of Kumbha

'Animals and humans, they are alike. All they need is kindness. A gentle pat, a loving word...these will do. You say Chunee of Kumbha killed a man. No animal kills without a reason. What

Tara Bai was right, of course. What Chunee needed was someone who loved him. Instead, he had a keeper who seemed to delight in troubling him. In 1815, a keeper named George Dyer was given charge of Chunee. There were reports that Dyer ill-treated the elephant.

was Chunee's reason? Was he shown the kindness he needed? Was there someone who whispered gentle words in his ears and gave him secret treats?

People say we, of Kumbha, have a magical touch with the elephants, that they listen to us and follow us. The truth is that when we look at the elephant, we see a creature that deserves love. That is why our birds sing sweeter, the milk our goats give us is thicker, and no elephant has killed one of us.

Wise words indeed! George Dyer, Chunee's keeper, had not understood this. And Chunee punished him for his cruelty. George Dyer's room was just above Chunee's cage. One day, Chunee broke through the roof and finding Dyer's clothes, destroyed them. There were even reports that he had eaten some of the clothes!

I have heard stories of how the sahibs treat their animals. You shout at them, and you poke and prod them with sharp spears. An animal that has seen anger, learns to show anger. It is the simplest rule in the world. And that is what Chunee did.'

Sujan, Mani, Surti, Bindi and Sundari – a few of the children of Kumbha

'Elephants are friendly and fun. They make the best friends. We have had many elephant friends.

The keepers were not the only ones who were cruel to the animals. The visitors to menageries came prepared to play ugly pranks on the animals. A man squirted a syringeful of vinegar into a lion's face while another used his penknife to wound an elephant's trunk. One man cut a lion's paw with a knife, while a bunch of college students thought it funny to throw firecrackers into the cages of the animals.

All they ever wanted was a lot of open space. Did you give your elephants the space they needed?

Elephants don't need much looking after. All you have to do is set them free among the trees. They will find their own food and not trouble you at all. If you don't want them to run away, you will need a fence around them. But our elephants never ran away from us. They put in their trunks through open windows and tickled us awake when they wanted someone to play with. They picked us up in their trunks and put us on their backs when they wanted to go to the river. Did you also play with your elephants?

They like to play hide-and-seek, they like to throw things and catch them. But you must be able to think of new games for them because elephants get bored very quickly. John Sahib says that the people of his country don't know how to do these things. They need to be taught what to do and how to do it.

Poor Chunee had very few friends in England. To the people in the menagerie, he was simply an animal that attracted large crowds and earned the owner a lot of money. John Taylor, who was Chunee's keeper for some time, was a good friend to the elephant. He taught Chunee to ring a bell to announce feeding time. He seemed to have understood what the elephant wanted and Chunee lost a good friend when the keeper left the menagerie. At the heart of the problem was the fact that Chunee was kept locked in a cage that was too small for him. There was no room for the elephant to move around comfortably.

Maybe you should send the men who care for elephants there, to Kumbha. We can show them how to care for elephants and how to keep them happy so that they will never hurt another human again.'

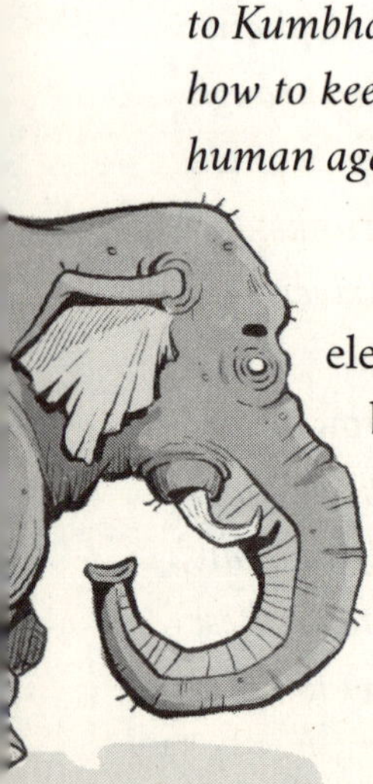

Before you pass judgement on Chunee the elephant, I beg you will consider the points raised by these people who know animals so well. Is the death of John Tietjen the elephant's fault?

I remain,
Your servant,
John Stebbling

Chunee had spent enough time with humans to recognize that he had made a mistake. The people who witnessed the death of John Tietjen reported that as soon as Chunee realized what he had done, he hrew down the spear, with which he had unintentionally wounded and killed the keeper. Then he stood there, shivering in fear at the terrible deed he had committed.

Qs and As

Did Chunee really kill his keeper?

Yes, he did. But it was not a result of his bad temper or anger. It was an accident. Tietjen was cleaning Chunee's cage. He usually carried a 12-foot-long spear to control the elephant. On that day, though, he decided that he didn't need it and threw it on the ground. Chunee picked it up and while twirling it around, accidentally killed his keeper.

What was the verdict of the coroner?

The coroner went to the menagerie and saw Chunee there. The elephant showed no signs of rage and this convinced the coroner to give a verdict of accidental death. Chunee was fined one shilling.

Were such accidents common in menageries?

Oh, yes. People were injured, sometimes fatally. Several lost their fingers. Ignorance was the primary reason for these accidents. The people of England, never having seen these animals before, didn't understand that these were wild animals that needed to be approached with caution. As a result, they thrust their hands into cages or reached out to pet the animals. A keeper who entered a lion's cage when it was sleeping, was attacked by the startled animal. People who teased the animals were also injured when the animals turned on them. At one of the travelling menageries, a boy who teased an elephant by feeding it stones instead of nuts was crushed by the irritated animal.

The crowd in the menageries also led to such accidents. A young boy visiting the Exeter Exchange menagerie was startled by the tiger's roar and, stepping backwards, fell on the monkey cage. The monkeys grabbed his hair, tugging at it and causing him serious injury. At a crowded venue, a man who was pushed close to the cage of the lioness, was grabbed by the animal and scratched badly.

Strange but True

George Stubbs, a painter of the age, once received news that there was a dead tiger at the menagerie. Stubbs hurried to the menagerie to buy the body which he then studied at great length. His painting of Pidcock's rhinoceros, and another titled *Cheetah and Stag with Two Indians*, are famous.

George Stubbs's stunning painting of an Indian rhinoceros is part of the collection of the Hunterian Museum in the Royal College of Surgeons of England in London. *Photo © By permission of the Hunterian Collection Trustees*

THE 'TIGER' THAT SWALLOWED A BOY

In nineteenth-century, England, the story of 'The Boy Who Was Swallowed by a Tiger' became very famous. The tigress of the real-life story belonged to Charles Jamrach, one of the best-known animal dealers of London. And well, fortunately the boy wasn't really 'swallowed'.

The year was 1857, and Charles Jamrach was in his shop near the London docks as usual. He was unloading a fresh delivery of animals. Among these was a large Bengal tigress. The tigress managed to break out of the box and escaped. Out on the road, she was seen by a boy.

The boy, who had never ever seen a tiger before, thought she was a large dog and put out his hand to pet her!

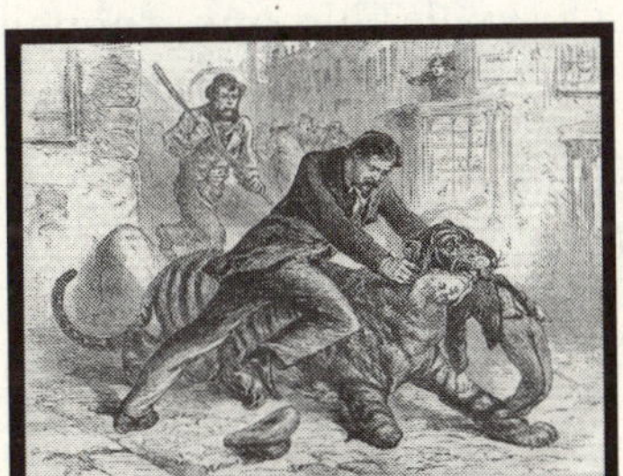

The tigress at once knocked the boy down and grabbing him by his shoulder, began to drag him away. Jamrach bravely fought off the tigress and saved the boy. With the help of his keepers, he was able to turn the tigress around towards his shop and trap her.

Miraculously, the boy sustained only a few scratches, which were soon treated. The boy's father then sued Jamrach, accusing him of negligence. The animal dealer was directed by the court to pay the boy 60 pounds.

The animal was sold off to a travelling menagerie where she gained fame as the tigress who 'swallowed the boy'. This incident was commemorated at Tobacco Dock, Wapping, London, with a statue depicting a boy staring at a large tigress.

7

ARE THERE BUN SHOPS IN THE JUNGLES OF INDIA?

The Zoological Society of London was set up by a group of people who believed that animals deserved open spaces, where people could see them. And so, the Regent's Park Zoo (also called London Zoo) opened its doors to the public in 1828. But in the early days of the zoo's existence, there were glaring problems in the way the animals were taken care of. The most important of these was about what the animals were fed. Visitors were encouraged to feed the animals and the wife of a keeper was allowed to sell buns in the zoo.

Did this food really suit the animals? No one stopped to consider this, except a perceptive young girl, who asked this very pertinent question.

10 September 1831
To the Regent's Park Zoo,
Please can you tell me, are there bun shops in the jungles of India?

I am sure you would like to know why I have asked you this question. My name is Sarah and my father is Keeper Michael at your zoo. He takes care of the birds in the zoo. Last week my father came home after work and asked my mother to make cakes and buns. When I woke up the next morning, the house smelt wonderfully of baking. All I wanted was a cake, warm from the oven. But when I tried to take one, what do you think Mother did? She slapped my hand away. These are not for you, she told me. I was upset. But I said nothing because I was certain I would get two cakes the next time Mother baked.

As we have seen from the previous stories, animals were displayed indoors for most of the eigheenth century and part of the nineteenth century in England. In 1826, a group of people led by Sir Stamford Raffles formed the Zoological Society of London and set up a zoo in Regent's Park. Visitors not only enjoyed the well-planned gardens but also had an opportunity to see exotic wild animals.

My mother baked again the next day. And the next. She baked cakes and buns every day for the next week. As soon as they were all done, she arranged them neatly in a basket. Sometimes, there were so many that they seemed in danger of spilling out. But my mother still refused to give me one to eat. What was more, she would not tell me where she was taking the sweet-smelling hamper. All I knew was that she left home with it full of the baked goodies. When she returned, the basket was empty, and her purse was heavy and clinked with coins. After a week of this, I did the only thing I could to satisfy my curiosity. I followed my mother.

Imagine my surprise when she walked across the city and straight into the zoo! Surely she was not taking the cakes and buns for Father? Mother walked through the gates, but I was stopped and asked to pay the admission fee.

In the early days, the zoo was not open to the public. In order to visit the zoo, Sarah would have needed a written order from a member of the Zoological Society. In addition, she would have had to pay one shilling to enter the zoo. On a Sunday, she would not have been allowed to enter because the zoo was open only to members on that day.

I had no money, and for a few minutes, I was afraid I would have to go home without finding out what Mother was doing in the zoo. Luckily for me, Keeper James saw me. He is a friend of Father's and knows me well. He takes care of the monkeys and always has funny stories to tell about them. He is a very nice man, and after he had explained things at the gate, I was allowed in.

The first animals given to the Zoological Society were a vulture, an eagle and a deer. Slowly, the zoo added to its collection by buying animals from around the world. All the animals were kept in heated rooms because people thought that they could not survive the cold in England. Statistics proved, however, that locking these animals in small, stuffy cages was not good for their health since the big cats only lived for around two years. This was when the new idea of keeping them in the fresh air without any artificial heating was adopted.

I had been to the zoo only once before, when it was first opened. It had seemed wide and empty then. Now there were more cages and crowds of people walking around.

It took me some time to find my mother. At last I saw her – standing close to the elephant. That surprised me. Even though Father works at the zoo, Mother doesn't really like animals. I've never seen her pet a cat, and she thinks dogs are dirty creatures and always shoos them away. I was even more surprised when I heard her ask the visitors to buy a bun for Jack.

Jack? I wondered: Who was Jack? Then I remembered Father telling me about the new elephant at the zoo.

Father had been very excited about the new animal and had even gone to the East India docks to receive him. The elephant had been too big to put into a van, so Father had walked him all the way to the zoo. Hadn't people stared, I asked my father. Of course they had, Father said. They had asked him questions about the animal, and children had run behind them. But Father had not

As you can see, the elephant in the zoo had a name. Contrast this with the early days of the menageries when animals lived and died without ever being named. Of course, it is possible that this was the name given to the elephant by his previous owner. But the animals in the zoo, particularly the large ones, were always given a name.

Interestingly though, the animals were given English names. When Jack died, a female elephant was purchased in Kanpur and brought to England. The elephant was called Katimah, but she was renamed Betsey and her calf was named Butcher.

minded. He was certain the news about a new elephant at the zoo would bring people rushing to see it. And it had. But I had never expected that my mother would be one among the people crowding the zoo to see the elephant!

> An elephant was an essential attraction to bring visitors to the zoo. And so, the Zoological Society of London bought one in 1831. This was an Indian elephant that had belonged to a Captain Smith and had lived with him in Madras (now Chennai, Tamil Nadu). Jack the elephant was 11 years old, a magnificent tusker and the largest elephant in Europe. The zoo paid 420 pounds for him.

'A bun for the elephant?' I heard Mother ask.

Many people bought Mother's buns and cakes. They held them out to the elephant and Jack's trunk snaked out at once, wrapped around the bun and carried it neatly to his mouth. Jack seemed to like the buns and cakes my mother baked. He did not refuse a single one, and always picked the food from people's hands with gentle care.

My mother was busy handing out the goodies and putting the money people gave her into her purse. She didn't see me until I was standing beside her. Then she stared in surprise at me. But before she could ask me what

I was doing there, I asked her my question: Are there bun shops in the jungles of India?

If you had been anywhere near the bears, you would probably have heard someone asking: 'A bun for the bears?' The bears were not housed in cages. Instead, they were kept in a deep pit with a thick post in the middle. When visitors appeared, the bears climbed the trunk. The visitors bought buns, cakes, nuts and fruits from the vendor nearby and fed the animals.

Of course not, Mother snapped. There was no bun shop in any jungle in India. Then where, I asked her, did elephants go to get buns and cakes? Mother told me I was being very silly because elephants ate grass and leaves and sugar cane. And whatever fruits they could find. Not cakes and buns from a shop.

Then why, I asked her, are you giving Jack buns and cakes? Won't they make him sick?

Mother did not like my questions. Some of the visitors were listening and Mother liked that even less. She got very huffy. If I

The eagerness with which Jack ate baked treats may fool you into thinking that perhaps the elephant was not fed well. Take a look at what Jack ate in a day: one-and-a-half large bundles of hay, 42 pounds of turnips, 3 pounds of boiled rice, bran, chaff, 10 pounds of biscuits, the straw meant for his bedding, and 36 buckets of water. The keepers tried to cut down on his food by giving him only a little light food on Sundays. But Jack protested so much that they were forced to feed him in the middle of the night and this fasting had to be given up.

had any questions, she hissed at me, I could ask the people who ran the zoo, not the woman selling buns and cakes for the elephant.

Sarah's question would have surprised many people, including those who cared for the wild animals. Most of them saw nothing wrong in feeding the animals food that humans ate. In fact, the director of Birmingham Zoological Gardens requested bakers who had stale bread to send it to the zoo for the bears and elephants. He hoped to bring down the food bills this way!

GARDENS OF THE ZOO

A bird's-eye view of the Regent's Park Zoo

AL SOCIETY, REGENT'S PARK.

Sarah's question was very valid. And yet, very few people considered it while offering food to the animals. People carried fruits, nuts and other treats to the zoo. Sometimes, they gave elephants tobacco or even wine, to see how they would react. So they thought nothing of buying a bun to feed the elephant or the bear. A cartoon published in the magazine *Punch* in 1871 highlighted the pathetic condition of zoo animals, particularly after a holiday. The cartoon showed a bunch of ill-looking animals after a holiday. A bear was complaining that 31,457 people had visited the zoo and they had given him 31,457 buns. Animals, it appears, were fed anything and everything. Consider the case of an elephant named Tom, who was brought over from Calcutta. Tom ate hay, corn, grass, wood shavings, rice, paper, straw, tea leaves, blacking, beer and champagne. There were other cases of animals known to be herbivores, being fed meat.

So, now you know the reason for this letter. If Jack ate leaves and grass in India, why do you let people feed him cakes and buns here? If buns and cakes were good for elephants, there would be a shop selling those in the forest. Please tell me this: Are there bun shops in the jungles of India?

Yours truly,

Sarah Trimble,

Daughter of Keeper Michael and Rose, the lady who sells cakes and buns.

Qs and As

Did the zoo really sell buns and cakes?

Oh, yes, they did. The Regent's Park Zoo bought Jack the elephant in 1831. Although the big cats were locked up in their cages, Jack was allowed to wander around the gardens. Children were given rides on the elephant and visitors were allowed to pet the animal. From here, it was only a short step to letting them feed the elephant. The wife of a keeper was asked to sell cakes and buns that the visitors could buy to feed Jack. This idea was very successful and feeding the elephant became a part of the experience of visiting the zoo. However, a visitor who took a bite of a bun was horrified to find it stale and tasteless, and wondered how this could be considered a treat for the animals.

How did the animals react to food of this kind?

While animals like elephants and bears seemed capable of digesting food of this kind, others often fell ill. A rare bird – the cassowary – was fed bread, apples and pears, and died. A chimpanzee performing for people on the streets of France was fed so many sweets by the spectators that it died because of the rich diet.

Strange but True

The people who worked with animals, took care of them and displayed them to the public, were dealing with animals from other countries. They had no idea how best to care for these creatures. Gilbert Pidcock's rhinoceros was fed clover and greens. But it was also given large quantities of biscuits. In addition, it was allowed to drink three to four bottles of sweet wine in a day! There are accounts of herbivores being fed sausages and beer in the morning, and cheese sandwiches in the day along with boiled potatoes and mutton.

8

WHY DIDN'T THE TIGERS ROAR?

Tigers and lions roaring ferociously, elephants salaaming endlessly and bears that danced without a break. This is what the public expected from the animals they viewed in menageries and the zoo. In menageries, the animals were often poked and prodded so they would roar. After all, that's how people expected the wild animals to behave. So, when the Prince of Wales returned from India with a host of animals, people gathered to hear the savage roars of the tigers. But they were disappointed because the animals did not make any sound. Most people felt cheated and were upset with the animals. It was only this young boy, who stopped to wonder why the tigers had not roared!

6 May 1876
Dear Regent's Park Zoo,
I have had a most tiring night and I blame it all on the Prince of Wales. My older sister Eliza is horrified that I would dare to blame a member of the royal family. It's not his fault, she told me. But it is! Why did he have to go on a tour of India? Eliza explained that this was because the Prince of Wales was now a prince of India too. And in a few years, he would be the king of England and of India too.

That was all very well. But did the Prince of Wales have to go on so many hunts in India? Eliza said that was what the members of the royal family did in their free

> When the English first came to India, they came as traders. They set up the East India Company to do business with India. Slowly, the company became more and more powerful, and set up factories in different parts of the country. They employed sepoys to protect their business interests. In 1857, the Indian sepoys rose against the English. After this uprising was suppressed, India was no longer in the hands of the company. Instead, it became a part of the British Empire. That's how the Prince of Wales became a prince of India too.

time. That was why the prince spent so many months in India. And why he travelled to all those places around India and hunted everywhere he went. All I can say is that the royal family seems to have too much time off.

The newspapers have been full of details of the prince's travels – where he went, what he did there and the people he met.

Albert Edward, the Prince of Wales, was the first member of the British royal family to visit India after it became a part of the British Empire. And so, the people of England were eager to know every last detail of the royal visit. Newspapers carried regular reports of what the prince was doing.

Of course, there were details of how many animals he hunted and pictures of the prince surrounded by many men. Some of them wore hats and some had cloth wound around their heads. And not one of them was smiling. The lower part of every photograph was full of the dead animals. There were deer and elephants and tigers, all laid out neatly on the ground, as if asleep. All I could think was how absolutely still those animals lay, and feel sad that they would never roar or walk through the jungle or simply enjoy the warmth of the sun.

All my brother Robert could do was marvel at the prince. He even kept a tally of all the animals the prince shot in India. It was Robert who knew about the Wild Beast Train and told us about it. All the animals that had been captured alive and the animals that had been gifted to the prince were being brought back to England.

Every Indian ruler who met the Prince of Wales had a gift for him. Many of these were expensive items made of precious metals. In addition to this, the prince was also gifted animals. Many of these came from the ruler of Nepal. Fortunately, there were three ships that were part of the prince's entourage – *Serapis*, *Raleigh* and *Osborne*. So there was plenty of space for everything!

They would be on this train called the Wild Beast Train since it was going to transport the wild animals from the jungles of India. Robert wanted to welcome the train when it arrived at the railway station. I don't know what my sister Eliza thought of this, but I was not interested in the train or the animals on it and would gladly have stayed home.

Why didn't you say so earlier, Eliza demanded.

But I hadn't, and so I had to go to Willow Walk Station with the rest of my family. The train was expected to reach the station in the evening.

Clarence Bartlett, from the Regent's Park Zoo, had accompanied the prince on this tour. He had taken care of the live animals and helped preserve the skins of the animals the prince had shot. Bartlett hoped to reach London by evening so that the animals could be settled in the zoo by nightfall.

However, Robert was so eager to see it and so scared that we would miss it that he hurried us along so that we left home at four o'clock. The sun was still out in the sky and it was a lovely evening. But Robert didn't let us look at the beautiful clouds or enjoy the gentle breeze. On the way to the railway station, Robert talked about the tigers.

To many people of England, India meant tigers and elephants. There was something about the ferocious tiger that touched the imagination of the English public and made them eager to see this animal.

There were four tigers, he said, and a tiger cub too. Robert even knew the names of these animals. Motee and Jahan were fully grown tigresses.

These two tigresses had been gifted to the prince by Sir Jung Bahadur, the ruler of Nepal, and were fierce animals. A sailor, trying to be friendly with them, had had a finger bitten off.

Tom and Minnie were young animals. The fifth was a cub that the sailors called Vixen because all it did was to snarl at everyone.

Tom and Minnie had been born in captivity and were used to humans. The sailors walked them up the ramp to the ship.

The prince was bringing back four elephants too.

Two of the elephants had been gifts from Sir Jung Bahadur. One was called Safar Kulley and the other was Jung Pershad. The sailors, who seem to have enjoyed having the animals on the ship, taught Jung Pershad to dance!

From the way he talked about the elephants, I knew my brother was dreaming of getting a ride on at least one of them.

> The elephants were not on the Wild Beast Train at all! Clarence Bartlett had realized that they were too big for the vans and so had sent them by road. The two elephants, their mahouts and keepers, completed the journey to the zoo in two days.

At the railway station, there was already a big crowd waiting. There were lots of men, a few women and many children. All the men could talk about was tigers and elephants and leopards.

More and more people came, and soon there was no room on the platform. Someone poked me in the ribs and another person stepped heavily on my toes. Eliza wondered if we could wait outside the railway station. Robert was horrified at the idea. What if we could not get back to the platform and missed seeing the animals? We understood then that he wanted to continue waiting at the platform.

All I wanted was to go home.

The Prince of Wales had brought back a cheetah called Phool Jharri, who was supposed to be beautiful and dangerous. Pompey was a young leopard who was born in Calcutta Zoo, and was tame and playful. The sailors enjoyed playing with a leopard named Jacko but complained that he had a scary scream. Lizzie was a quiet young leopard, but her brother Sailor could be dangerous. He had damaged Lizzie's ear, and used his sharp claws to tear the trousers of a sailor walking past him.

You should have said something, my sister said.

The Wild Beast Train finally limped into the station around 10 p.m. There had been reports of it being delayed, and – later – news about the engine breaking down.

Many things went wrong with the transportation of animals from the ship to the train. For one thing, the tigers refused to leave their cages. Finally, fireworks were used to scare them so they could be moved into the train. As a result, the loading of the animals took longer than expected and the train carrying them was delayed.

People around me discussed these delays but I paid no attention to them. All I knew was that I had stood at this platform for hours and never wanted to see it again. All I knew was that everyone here thought the Prince of Wales had been very brave in India and was proud of him. All I knew was that it was long past my bedtime, my legs ached, and I wanted some peace and quiet.

You really should have said something, Eliza said.

From these accounts, it sounds like the prince had faced all the wild animals alone and managed to shoot them in the face of danger. The truth was that when the British set out on shikars, they usually had a large team to take care of them. The prince's shikar in Nepal had 4,000 camp followers, 600 camels and 163 elephants. And of course, members of his own team.

There was no time to say anything. The train steamed into the railway station, groaning and clanking. There was immediate excitement among the waiting people. They pushed and shoved and craned their necks to see the animals. Babies were lifted on to their fathers' shoulders and children stood on their toes, trying to peer over the sea of heads. Then, finally, the carriage doors opened. Silence fell on the platform as the cages were unloaded. But there was nothing to see! The cages were all covered in canvas.

But still people waited, hoping to at least hear something. *Anything*. A roar perhaps, or a growl. Even a snarl would have pleased the waiting crowd. But the only noise on that railway platform was the rough scraping of the cages being pulled, and the grunts and orders of the men unloading them. As for the animals, they said nothing.

Actually, the animals did make some noises. Minnie gave something between a grunt and a yawn when her cage was lifted, Vixen was heard hissing and Phool Jharri gave a sharp, short growl. However, these were probably not heard by the people. And in any case, these were not the loud roars that the people were expecting to hear.

Why didn't the tigers roar, a newspaper wondered the next day. The reporter talked about the people who had waited so patiently for hours, children who had gone home disappointed because they had not seen a single wild animal. No one remembered that these animals had been snatched from their homes. Or that they had been trapped and captured. Some of them had watched their mother die. They had been dragged away from their mother's side and pushed into boxes that were too small for them to stand or sit comfortably. They had travelled on carts or camel-back to the port. Then they had made the long journey by ship, and then on a clanging, whistling train. They were scared and uncomfortable and confused. They deserved to be left alone. They needed peace and quiet.

Just like I needed my bed.

I wish, Eliza wailed, you had said something.

I didn't mind not saying anything for myself. But I have to say this now. It was wrong to threaten and scare these animals. It was heartless to send them on a journey they didn't want. It was selfish to expect them to roar just to satisfy us.

If I don't want to do things that don't make me happy, why should these animals?

I remain,

Yours sincerely,

Edward Turnbull

Qs and As

Why did the Prince of Wales go to India?

This visit was meant to strengthen the relations between the people of the two countries. The prince met the rulers of various princely states in India.

What did the Prince of Wales bring back from India?

The prince was an important guest. After all, he was the future ruler of India. And so, he was given many items of great value by the Indian rulers. These were later exhibited in the India Museum in London, and attracted large crowds.

The rulers of India also gave the prince many animals and birds to take back to England. Most of these were given to the Regent's Park Zoo and people flocked to see them.

The Prince of Wales brought back 16 tiger skins. These were the animals that he had shot on his shikars in different parts of India. These had been treated and cured by Clarence Bartlett. Each of these had the date when the animal had been shot affixed to it. He also brought back the feet of an elephant that he had shot in Ceylon (now Sri Lanka).

The three ships also carried the 151 animals that the prince was bringing back. Of these, 65 were mammals and 86 were birds.

Here is a list of the animals brought back from India:

2 green monkeys	4 tailless dogs
2 rhesus monkeys	3 Tibetan mastiffs
5 tigers	2 white dogs
7 leopards	2 Indian white dogs
1 cheetah	1 Himalayan bear
1 viverrine cat	4 Indian elephants
1 Indian civet	6 domestic sheep
2 musk deer	4 shawl goats
2 Thar goats	2 zebus
8 antelopes	3 axis deer
2 spotted porcine deer	

Strange but True

Abraham Dee Bartlett, the director of the Regent's Park Zoo, used a travelling cage to move the animals to new locations. This consisted of a narrow cage that was attached to the open door of the animal's cage. Food was offered as temptation to get the animal into the travelling cage. Once the animal was in there, the door was slammed shut. Now the travelling cage was hoisted onto a trolley and moved to the new location.

9

WHAT HAPPENED TO THE PRINCE'S LEOPARD?

The news that the Prince of Wales was visiting India sent the rajas, British officials, army staff, tea planters and businessmen into a tizzy. How could they honour the royal visitor and what could they gift him? The men of the 109th regiment of the Indian army, eager to impress the prince, gifted him a leopard. Neither these men nor the prince knew where the leopard had come from, or imagined for a minute that it might be missed there. But as this letter from the children of a village proves, the bond with the creatures who share your world cannot be easily forgotten!

25 September 1876

Dear Sahib who takes care of the animals,

Please accept our sincere namaskars.

We are the children of a village named Bumrah. You are not likely to have heard of it because Bumrah has nothing to boast of. It has no famous buildings and no sacred river. People say Bumrah is a small village. But we think it is just right. There is nothing to see in Bumrah, others complain. But for us, the thick jungle that lies beyond Bumrah is our playground and there's always something to do there. There are dried branches to gather and fruit to pick. We know the animals that make their homes here, and they know us.

Everyone in the village wears a friendly smile and so, when strangers appeared one day, people noticed them at once. They came at the beginning of the cold season and there were three of them. We saw at once that they were hunters. They were looking for an animal, they said. Not just any ordinary animal. They wanted an animal that they could trap and gift to a prince.

Animals were considered the best thing to gift someone you wanted to please. The kings and nawabs of India often sent elephants, tigers or exotic birds all the way to England. For officials of the East India Company too, sending an animal to please a member of the British royal family was very common.

That is how we learnt that a prince from a faraway land was coming. He liked animals, the hunters said. They didn't stop to tell us more but stepped in amid the trees of the jungle and melted into the shadows there.

There was great excitement in the village. Knots of anxious people gathered to discuss how they could ask the prince for help. People like Bhole Nath, whose cow had been stolen by his cousin Ram Singh, decided to petition the prince to get it back.

The people of India had great faith in the power of princes, kings and rajas to settle disputes. Everywhere the Prince of Wales went, he met people who brought petitions for him to settle. The truth, of course, was that the prince had little knowledge or understanding of the situation in India.

There were others who wanted to see the preparations in Patna (now in Bihar) to welcome the prince. They were busy making plans to travel to the big city. But these things did not interest us. All we wanted to know was what the hunters were doing in our jungle.

They were gone for a whole day and night. When they stepped out of the jungle, we were there, waiting.

The people of India gave the Prince of Wales a grand welcome. All the cities he visited were lit up with thousands of lamps. The most important people of each kingdom met him and offered gifts of all kinds. Colourful parades and grand dinners were organized in his honour.

While we did that, we wondered which animal the hunters would trap. There was a herd of elephants that came sometimes, rustling and crashing mightily among the trees. There were plenty of deer, and some big cats that wove among the trees as gently as the sun did in the

The people of any Indian village always knew of the animals that lived in the jungles around them. But they seldom attacked these animals or even attempted to hunt them. Sometimes, a boar got into the fields and destroyed the crops. Or a tiger began to steal cows from various herds. At such times, the villagers got together to find a solution. But because very few of them owned firearms, they had to seek the help of the Englishmen if there was no way out but to kill the animals.

clouds. But the hunters had not caught any of these. They had caught the leopard.

The leopard, you must understand, is not our friend. Such animals never are. But you cannot sip from the same stream and be enemies. That was how it was with the leopard. We had seen it often, crouched among the bushes or slaking its thirst at the river. And often, as we wandered among the trees, we had felt its gaze upon us, curious and watchful. The leopard could have attacked us any time it wanted to. But it chose not to.

It may be difficult to believe, but not every animal attacked humans in the jungle. The shikaris who hunted in the forests had many stories to tell of animals that slunk by very close to them, without bothering to attack them.

So, now, when we saw it with its feet tied and strung upside down on a pole, we chose to fight for it. We asked the hunters to let it go. We told them of other animals they could give the prince, the deer and the nilgai, or the bears that lived in a cave at the foot of a distant hill and were no one's friends. We even told them of the tiger in the next village. It was a man-eater, so they would also

A tiger that killed and ate humans was called a man-eater. These animals were dangerous, and terrified villagers often moved away from their homes when there was one nearby. The British government announced rewards for killing a man-eater, and often enthusiastic hunters set out to win the money.

get the reward the government had placed as bounty on its head.

However, the hunters refused to let the leopard go. We had no cause to worry about the animal, they told us. The prince was rich enough to create a forest only for it. The leopard, they said, would rule this jungle. We watched them carry the leopard away, the animal snarling with rage.

We heard later that the prince was pleased with the leopard, that he nodded and smiled as he accepted it. The leopard too, people said, had recognized its master and known him for a great man. Why else had the leopard bowed to the prince?

We did not see any of this. We did not leave Bumrah when many others travelled to the big city. We stayed and wandered the forest paths as we had always done. But it was not like it had always been. All we saw now was the

It is difficult to believe that a leopard bowed to a prince or even recognized him as its master. The leopard, furious at being captured and put into a small cage, is more likely to have roared in rage!

emptiness that the leopard had left behind. We saw all the places it was no longer seen. We heard little rustles and secretive movements, which were not made by it. And that is why we are writing to you. We want to know how it is, the leopard of Bumrah.

The sahibs in the city said you would have answers to all our questions. Has the prince given the leopard open spaces to run? Are there stands of thick-trunked trees for it to sharpen its claws? Is there a swift river where the

leopard can quench its thirst? Do the trees cast dark pools of shade where the leopard can hide? Please tell us: What happened to the prince's leopard?

We remain,
Your very obedient servants,
Kishan, Murari, Teej Bai, Rani
and Kallu Ram

Many of the animals that were captured in India died. While some of them died on the journey to the port, for others the voyage on the ship proved disastrous. Still others could not get used to a new climate and died. There were many reasons for the death of animals. But sadly, these deaths rarely upset people. The British government was confident that India, now a part of the British Empire, could always be relied upon to supply more animals.

Qs and As

Is this the same prince that we met in the previous story?

Yes, this was the same one – Albert Edward, the Prince of Wales. He was on a tour of the Bengal Presidency where the soldiers of a regiment gifted him a leopard.

What happened to the animals the prince collected on his India trip?

As we know, the prince took all the animals he had been gifted back to England with him. Remember that before the animals were taken on board the three ships, they had to make a long overland journey. The voyage was also a great challenge and not all animals survived it. A four-horned deer jumped off the ship and drowned. A rare deer that survived the voyage was loaded into a van of the Wild Beast Train at Portsmouth. Someone, eager to get a glimpse of the animal, opened the van and the deer leapt out. It was later found dead on the railway track.

The other animals were taken to the Regent's Park Zoo, with most being gifted to the facility. Only a few of them were retained by the prince. Even these were housed in the zoo until the prince wanted them.

These were some of the animals presented by the Prince of Wales to the Regent's Park Zoo:

2 tigers

2 leopards

1 elephant

2 antelope

Jung Pershad, the elephant gifted by the ruler of Nepal, was given on loan to the zoo. He stayed in the Regent's Park Zoo till his death in 1896. The other two elephants, Omar and Rustom, stayed in the zoo till 1882. They were then presented to the zoological garden in Berlin, Germany.

10

WHY DID THE TIGER CUB HATE THE PRINCE?

Shikar was considered a part of the Indian experience and people travelling to India from England came prepared for it. The market was flooded with books written by experienced British shikaris, offering suggestions on how to hunt in India. Over time, some of these people turned away from hunting and accepted the need to protect animals. For many of them, the turning point came when they saw the agony that the animals suffered. This forced them to agree that animals too experienced the same emotions that humans did.

On the journey from India to England, the people on the ships noticed that a tiger cub named Vixen hated the Prince of Wales. But it was left to these children to ask questions about why the animal hated the prince so much.

25 June 1876

Dear Director of the Regent's Park Zoo,

Our father is a sailor. And a few days ago, he returned from a long voyage. Do you know where he went? He travelled on the *Serapis,* the ship that carried the Prince of Wales to India and back!

Father came back with many stories about the prince. Then one day, Father told us about Minnie. He said Minnie had been a passenger on the *Serapis*. We wondered if she had been a woman or perhaps a young girl. But she was not a human. She was a tigress! You see, the prince had brought back many animals from his travels in India. And these animals travelled with him on the ship.

Minnie and her brother Tom, Father said, were tigers who had grown up with people. They played with the sailors and were always ready to learn new tricks. One of the sailors decided to give Minnie a bath. She hated it and always leapt in the air if she even heard the clank of a bucket!

> The voyage from India to England took weeks and, during this time, the sailors usually befriended the animals on board. They gave them names and spent their free time teaching them tricks.

Phool Jharri was a cheetah. Father said she was beautiful but very dangerous. There were two other young leopards, Pompey and Jacko, and they had been very friendly. Father had many stories about them, and they all made us squeal with laughter.

Father told us about the two elephants named Omar and Rustom. He said they were very talented and even helped the sailors on the voyage!

Omar and Rustom learnt how to help the sailors! The ship had furnaces that burnt coal. The ash from these furnaces had to be emptied and the two elephants were the ones who did this. At the words 'hoist away', they obediently pulled up the buckets and stopped as soon as they heard the words 'high enough'.

But it was the story about the tiger cub that the sailors called Vixen that we liked to hear. Father said this cub didn't gambol or play. Why, it didn't even want to leave its cage. Several sailors tried to be friendly with it. But the cub simply snarled at anyone who went too close to its cage. The sailors were unhappy and upset with this behaviour. That was until they saw how the cub reacted to the Prince of Wales. If the prince happened to be nearby, Vixen sprang furiously at the bars of the cage and roared hoarsely at the prince. Father said the cub bared its teeth in rage if it ever caught sight of the prince. Why, we wondered, did the tiger cub hate the prince?

We found out yesterday when Father took us to see the animals at the zoo. The prince's animals were all in a big enclosure. It had wooden sides and a canvas roof. And below this roof were many cages.

We walked around the enclosure, looking at the animals. And it was like meeting old friends! We looked at Tom and Minnie, and laughed at Jacko and Pompey.

Vixen lay in a corner of its cage, growling softly. There was no one in front of its cage and we saw at once that the cub was in a bad mood. It didn't come when we called and seemed not to recognize Father. We stared at the angry creature and wondered again: Why did it hate the

The animals brought by the Prince of Wales were exhibited for a few months and attracted a lot of attention. Queen Victoria, the Prince and Princess of Wales, and several members of the royal family visited the zoo to see the animals. Large crowds of the general public came too, and the zoo had a record 915,764 visitors in 1876. An estimated 215,846 more people visited the zoo in 1876, compared to the previous year.

prince? Father was surprised at our interest in the bad-tempered animal. He tried to take us away and show us the elephants and the bears.

'Mr Brown' was the name given to the bear in the Prince of Wales's collection. Mr Brown's mother had been killed by the prince. Perhaps this was the reason why Mr Brown was a moody animal, refusing to join in the fun with the sailors on board.

However, it was Vixen we wanted to look at, it was Vixen we wondered about. That was when Father told us the most interesting story of how the cub was caught and how it was brought on the *Serapis*. This story will help you understand why Vixen hates the prince.

High in the hills of Nepal (Father told us this is a place near India), the prince was out hunting one day. He saw a tigress and shot her. This was Vixen's mother. The hunting party saw at once that the tigress had cubs and knew they must be somewhere close by. Two soldiers were sent to look for the cubs. They found a cave and entered it. There was only one cub there, hiding in a corner. This was Vixen. Vixen put up a good fight and managed to scratch those soldiers badly. But could a small cub really fight and defeat two grown men? No, Father said, it could

not. And that's how Vixen was caught and carried off.

The first thing the cub saw was its mother, stretched out on the ground. The Prince of Wales was standing over the body. Is it surprising that Vixen hates the man who murdered its mother?

So, if the Prince of Wales should visit the zoo and ask to see his animals, you should show him the leopards and tigers and elephants. But, please, don't let him near Vixen. People will be sure to notice Vixen growling and roaring at the prince and wonder: Why does the tiger cub hate the prince?

We remain,

Yours sincerely,

Joseph and Jacqueline Brown

Beautifully he did shoot
Many a royal tiger brute.
Laying on their backs they die,
Shot in the apple of the eye.

– A poem about the royal sportsman in India

Qs and As

How was a tiger shot?

Tiger shooting was rarely a solo activity. The hunting party comprised a large number of people. These were usually shikaris from the nearby villages, who knew the area well. It was they who led the hunter to the spot where the tiger had been spotted.

The hunter could choose to shoot the tiger from a *machan*. This was a wooden platform built among the branches of a tree. A goat or cow was tied below the *machan*, as bait for the tiger. The hunter spent the night in the *machan*, waiting for the tiger to come so he could shoot it.

If the hunter wanted to enjoy a good chase, then he did not choose to sit in the *machan*. Instead, a large team of beaters got to work as soon as the tiger was spotted. They beat loudly on drums, and sometimes used fire, to drive the animal towards the hunters.

Many hunters preferred to hunt tigers from the back of elephants. They were able to look down on the grass and scrub, and spot the hiding tiger easily. There were others who thought that hunting a tiger on foot was the most courageous way to do it. This was daring because tigers often turned on the hunters and attacked unwary men. This made it difficult for the hunters to shoot them.

What happened to Vixen's mother after she was shot?

The first thing was to ensure that the animal was really dead. There were many stories of tigers that leapt up even after they had been shot. Once it was certain that the animal was dead, it was time to measure the tigress.

To do this, she would have been laid flat on the ground. Then a tape measure would have been held from her nose to the tip of her tail. Measuring a tiger was an important part of the whole shikar experience. Hunters liked to know the measurements of the animals they had just killed, how tall and how long they were. People also made records of the condition of the skin, teeth, and used these to guess the age of the animal.

Once this was done, the animal would have been skinned. Skinning meant peeling the tiger's skin off the body. This had to be done quickly, before the body of the tiger cooled down. Someone with experience of skinning an animal had to do this work. Otherwise, the skin would be ruined and could not be displayed by the hunter. The skin was treated with chemicals, to make sure that it did not rot. If the skin was not properly treated, the fur was likely to fall off. Details of when the tigress had been shot were fixed on the skin. Now it was ready to be displayed on the walls or floor of the Prince of Wales's home.

Did hunters always take the cubs of the animals that they killed?

Sometimes, they did. However, it was difficult for an Englishman to raise these in his house. There are stories of tiger cubs that turned violent when they grew older. In such cases, the young animals were given away to a zoo or menagerie. Cubs that had been orphaned were not likely to survive on their own and usually died.

Strange but True

The Zoological Society of London awarded the Prince of Wales its first gold medal for the generous donations of animals he had made to the zoo.

ACKNOWLEDGEMENTS

This book began with my desire to know more about the animals that were trapped and transported to England during the British Raj. It speedily turned me into a detective, as I consulted books and chased down references before making triumphant connections and forging important links. In the process of writing this book, I have had the support of a wonderful bunch of people.

I am grateful to the long-ago travellers, whose detailed accounts of travels between India and England brought the past so gloriously alive for me. I am in awe of all the contemporary authors, who have made it their life's mission to write about animals. Their books not only led me to other titles but also provided me with valuable insights into the field.

Thank you – to Vatsala Kaul Banerjee of Hachette India, for her enthusiastic response to the project.

Thank you – to the illustrator of this book, Damini Gupta, for her gorgeous illustrations.

To Pramod, for listening to all my ideas, answering questions and endlessly discussing British rule in India, a huge thank you. Your support, and faith in me, means more than I can say.

Aai and Baba, for their constant encouragement, thank you.

Daddy and Mummy, for their affectionate interest in my projects, thank you.

Kavita, for listening to my discussions of my work in progress, and for her unflagging enthusiasm, thank you.

Richa, for being my ready solver of all kinds of issues – moral, ethical, technological – thank you!

Dogma, Sandy, Tilak, Teddy – the dogs on my street, thank you. We humans truly don't deserve your love.

And Pranav, whose magic with cats and dogs fills me with joy, pride and hope – thank you.

SELECT BIBLIOGRAPHY

Altick, Richard. D. *The Shows of London*. Cambridge and London: Belknap Press, 1978.

Bartlett, A.D. *Bartlett's Life Among the Wild Beasts in the 'Zoo': Being a Continuation of Wild Animals in Captivity: The Habits, Food, Management and Treatment of the Beasts and Birds at the 'Zoo', with Reminiscences and Anecdotes*. London: Chapman and Hall, 1900.

Bartlett, A.D. *Wild Animals in Captivity: Being an Account of the Habits, Food, Management and Treatment of the Beasts and Birds at the 'Zoo', with Reminiscences and Anecdotes*. 2nd ed. London: Chapman and Hall, 1899.

Blunt, Wilfrid. *The Ark in the Park: The Zoo in the Nineteenth Century*. London: Hamish Hamilton, 1976.

Broderip, W.J. *Zoological Recreations*. 2nd ed. Philadelphia: Lea and Blanchard, 1849.

Clarke, T.H. *The Rhinoceros from Durer to Stubbs 1515–1799*. London: Sotheby's Publications, 1986.

Cowie, Helen. *Exhibiting Animals in Nineteenth-century Britain: Empathy, Education, Entertainment*. Basingstoke: Palgrave Macmillan, 2014.

Grigson, Caroline. *Menagerie: The History of Exotic Animals in England*. Oxford: Oxford University Press, 2016.

Landmann, George. *Adventure and Recollections of Colonel Landmann*. 2 vols. London: Colburn and Co., 1852.

MacKenzie, John. M. *The Empire of Nature: Hunting, Conservation and British Imperialism*. Manchester: Manchester University Press, 1988.

Plumb, Christopher. *Exotic Animals in Eighteenth-century Britain*. Unpub. Diss.

Ritvo, Harriet. *The Animal Estate: The English and Other Creatures in the Victorian Age*. Cambridge: Harvard University Press, 1987.

Robbins, Louise. E. *Elephant Slaves and Pampered Parrots: Exotic Animals in Eighteenth-century Paris*. Baltimore and London: Johns Hopkins University Press, 2002.

Russell, William Howard. *The Prince of Wales Tour, a Diary in India: With Some Account of the Visits of His Royal Highness to the Courts of Greece, Egypt, Spain and Portugal*. 2nd ed. London: Sampson Low, Marston, Searle & Rivington, 1877. Second Edition.

Scherren, Henry. *The Zoological Society of London: A Sketch of Its Foundation and Development and the Story of Its Farm, Museum, Gardens, Menagerie and Library*. London and Paris: Cassell and Company Limited, 1905.

Swainson, William. *Animals in Menageries*. London: Longman, Orme, Brown, Green & Longmans, 1838.

IMAGE COPYRIGHT INFORMATION

Page 13: Artist: Jacques-Laurent Agasse, 'The Nubian giraffe'; Wikimedia Commons Public Domain; Source: Royal Collection (UK) ID: 404394; **Pages 14–15:** Exeter Change in 1826: Wikimedia Commons, no restrictions; Publisher: London: Cassell, Petter, & Galpin; Contributing Library: University of California Libraries; Digitizing Sponsor: Internet Archive; **Page 30:** Artist: Alfred Thomas Elwes, 'A Wild-Beast Shop'; Wikimedia Commons Public Domain; This file is from the Mechanical Curator collection, a set of over 1 million images scanned from out-of-copyright books and released to Flickr Commons by the British Library, UK; **Page 31**: Poster of rhinoceros: from Collectanea: or, A collection of advertisements and paragraphs from the newspapers, relating to various subjects Publick exhibitions and places of amusement; Public Domain; held by British Library, UK; **Page 59:** 'The Menagerie in the Tower': New York Public Library Digital Collections 1660387; **Pages 60–61:** Royal Menagerie, Exeter 'Change, Strand; Creator: Thomas Rowlandson; Publisher: Rudolph Ackermann; Public Domain; held by British Library, UK; **Page 80:** Illustration for the magazine article 'The Old Elephant in Exeter 'Change', Once a Week volume 9, page 587. Source: Internet Archive; Wikimedia Commons Public Domain; **Page 81, top:** Chunees Skelett; Source: Jan Bondeson, *Animal Freaks*; Wikimedia Commons Public Domain; **Page 81, bottom:** Verkaufsanzeige für die Haut des Elefanten Chunee; Source: http://www.tokensociety.org.uk/articles/tokens/pidcocks.shtml; Wikimedia Commons Public Domain; **Page 83, top:** 'Jumbo and his keeper Matthew Scott giving a ride to children about the Zoo'; Source: from *Jumbo: This Being the True Story of the Greatest Elephant in the World* by Paul Chambers; Wikimedia Commons Public Domain; **Page 83, bottom:** Source: from *Jumbo: This Being the True Story of the Greatest Elephant in the World* by Paul Chambers; Wikimedia Commons Public Domain; **Page 94:** Rhinoceros (ca. 1780-91), oil on canvas, 69.9 x 92.7 cm, by George Stubbs; private collection of the Hunterian Museum in the Royal College of Surgeons of England in London. Photo © By permission of the Hunterian Collection Trustees; **Page 95:** Illustration for 'My Struggle with a Tiger' by Charles Jamrach, published in *The Boy's Own Paper* on 1 February 1879; **Pages 104–105:** Gardens of the Zoological Society, London, 1828; Wood engraving; Creator: J. Dodd; Public Domain; held by British Library, UK